NATIONAL COUNCIL
FOR
ENVIRONMENTAL BALANCE
P. O. Box 7732
Louisville, Kentucky 40207

WHY ARE THEY LYING TO OUR CHILDREN?

Also by Herbert I. London

Closing the Circle: A Cultural History of the Rock Revolution
The American Economy
Myths that Rule America
The Seventies: Counterfeit Decade
The Overheated Decade
Social Science Theories, Structures and Application (editor and
contributor)
Fitting In: Crosswise at the Generation Gap
Non-White Immigration and the White Australia Policy
Education in the Twenty-First Century

WHY ARE THEY LYING TO OUR CHILDREN?

Herbert I. London

Foreword by
Herman Kahn

𝔰𝔡

STEIN AND DAY/*Publishers*/New York

First published in 1984
Copyright © 1984 by The Hudson Institute
All rights reserved, Stein and Day, Incorporated
Designed by Louis A. Ditizio
Printed in the United States of America
STEIN AND DAY/*Publishers*
Scarborough House
Briarcliff Manor, N.Y. 10510

Library of Congress Cataloging in Publication Data
London, Herbert Ira.
   Why are they lying to our children?

   Bibliography: p.
   Includes index.
   1. Social prediction—United States. 2. Economic
forecasting—United States. 3. Quality of life—United
States—Forecasting. 4. Textbooks—United States. 5. Mass
media—United States. I. Title.
HM24.L78 1983   303.4′973   83-42975
ISBN 0-8128-2937-9

To Herman Kahn,
a giant intellectually
and an inspiration personally

Acknowledgments

I will take the blame for the excesses in this book. Where those excesses exist they are related to my emotional commitment to the problem of inadequate textbooks. However, many people deserve credit for this book. Herman Kahn was an inspiration. He was the one person I knew who was continually imaginative and generous with his ideas. Without him this book would not have been written. His recent death was a great loss to anyone concerned about intellectual integrity. Tom Bell, the president of The Hudson Institute and a person of rare insight, was the catalyst behind this project. Jane Newitt, a respected senior policy analyst and the author of an extended paper on the same theme, provided her research findings as the basis for my arguments. Audrey Tobin did so many research tasks, including obtaining the textbooks, that her contributions are too numerous to enumerate. Carol Kahn is a special editor and friend whose gentle manner and carefully couched criticism are greatly appreciated. To these people I offer my gratitude. I only hope I haven't embarrassed them with my arguments.

Contents

WHY ARE THEY LYING TO OUR CHILDREN?

Foreword

War, famine, environmental disasters, material shortages, and a declining quality of life—that's what schoolchildren are being taught to expect in their futures. What these grim and mostly inaccurate forecasts are doing to their lives I don't know for sure. But I do know this: Our children are absorbing excessively negative misinformation. In classrooms, in newspapers, and on television, children are being taught that the advanced, industrialized, capitalist nations (and especially the United States) are using up the Earth's resources and running out of energy; are carelessly and selfishly polluting the environment; are exploiting the poor "have-not" nations to enrich the "haves" even further; are eating too much artificial, additive-laden junk food while letting most of the world starve; and are sacrificing safety for profit in the exploitation of new technologies.

Just as significant as what our children are being taught is what they are *not* being taught: for example, that the wealthy nations play a constructive and essential role in furthering world economics;

that rapid economic growth has changed many non-Western nations from poor to middle-income status; that most resources are more accessible and less costly today than ever before; and that new forms of energy have been created. All these forms of progress are likely to proceed even more effectively in the future.

Much of what is being taught is misleading, often even just plain wrong. For example, almost all the textbooks that discuss the future refer to our "natural resources" as "dwindling" without ever explaining that not all resources are "natural" and that a resource doesn't necessarily "dwindle" even if we use a lot of it. Usually new methods of extraction are developed, new sources are discovered, or equally desirable substitutes are found. It is very important to recognize that a resource can be created or made usable by technology, capital, skill, and organization. As a result, most traditional resources and commodities are becoming more available, not less so. In addition, we now create many "unnatural" resources such as plastics, silicon chips, solar cells, and laser component systems, to name a few. Some of these new resources can be substituted quite effectively for old ones—we can, for example, substitute aluminum wire, glass fibers, microwaves, and satellites for copper in wires. A textbook reference to dwindling resources, therefore, is simply inadequate and misleading without a fuller explanation.

Another shortcoming of schools and textbooks is the lack of any attempt to put this bleak picture into a comparative framework. Although ours obviously is an imperfect world, it is a great deal less imperfect than it once was, as a look at the continuum of history demonstrates quite well. From a long-term perspective, mankind at present is about midway through a 300–400-year-long "great transition"—progressing from a time when human beings almost everywhere were relatively few, poor, and at the mercy of the forces of nature, to a time when they should be (barring some perverse combination of bad luck and bad management) almost everywhere numerous, rich, and largely in control of the forces of nature.

This kind of optimistic, future-oriented perspective is not new. Indeed, optimism (as well as pessimism) runs in cycles. It seems as though the pessimistic trend, however, is appearing with greater frequency; the pervasive economic, social, and political malaise with us since the mid-1960s is the fifth "down" time since Malthus. The quantitative and qualitative progress we've made—the material gains, increased life-spans, nutritional advances, scientific break-throughs, and so on—have become so taken for granted as to be ignored. Indeed, children who regard space shots and moon missions as standard television fare are unlikely to recognize the significance of the eight-hour workday—unless, of course, it is clearly pointed out to them. Without proper exposition and exposure, most of the evidence supporting a more positive outlook is simply lost.

The need for a more comprehensive and balanced perspective becomes increasingly clear as much of the contemporary conventional wisdom is recognized as incorrect. The highly publicized doomsday warnings of the *Limits to Growth* report, issued by the Club of Rome in 1972, were dubious at the time and now are almost completely proved wrong. In fact, the leaders of the club have publicly modified many of their excessively pessimistic assertions (for example, that the world is running out of resources), but not surprisingly, the revisions have been made without fanfare and received scant media attention.

Similarly, *The Global 2000 Report*, issued by the Carter administration in 1980, was inaccurate when it appeared and has become even more so since then, although its misleading conclusions are still quoted widely. But according to the report's own projections of per-capita income growth for the poorer countries, for example, there will be significant transfers of old technologies as well as revolutionary advances in technology. And even if such technological progress doesn't occur, the living standards of the world's populations, I believe, will continue to improve well past the year 2000.

We in North America, however, continue to believe the bleak prognoses. National surveys in the United States reveal a pervasive fear of pollution, resource limitations, and a general deterioration in the quality of life. Most parents believe their children will inherit a world less good than their own. Most children believe it, too.

Too bad, because the prospects are excellent for a rich, satisfying, and highly technological postindustrial society. Assuming that the current improvement in the economic situation continues (and it should, given a combination of cyclical forces, well-designed "fixes," and America's underlying strength), the United States should be able to attain a 3 or 4 percent average growth rate between 1980 and 2000. If this happens, the country's gross national product in the year 2000 will be about twice what it was in 1980, and the per-capita income will almost double, averaging more than $20,000 annually (calculated in 1980 dollars). Poverty, as defined by current criteria, virtually will have disappeared. There will always be a bottom 20 percent, but the bottom will become increasingly higher.

That's the good news. The bad news is that none of this is being taught in our schools. Some people believe this failing contributes to negative self-images, leading the children to do poorly in school, or to become troublemakers, or eventually to drop out of school and even society. One analyst of the contemporary scene recently was quoted as saying, "Suicide as a leading cause of death among young people may be due to depressing textbooks."

A less drastic assessment is that most young people are able to cope quite well simply by blending the grim view of United States and global prospects they receive in school with a natural optimism about their own futures. The comment "We feel we're traveling first class on the *Titanic*" exactly expresses their position. I suspect this youthful view is the more accurate one and that the harm being done by

14

society's negativism is not as severe as some might fear. But neither is it beneficial or conducive to imbuing our children with a sense of pride and good citizenship.

For this they need a more optimistic scenario of the future, and it should be presented by teachers who are well informed and familiar with current data and the constructive uses of affluence and technology. Young people need teachers who can help them distinguish emotional and biased arguments from factual ones and who can present objective reasons for the fact that our system is still very attractive to most people in most places.

With some exceptions, the texts and courses dealing with "futures" education are not of high quality, so it does not disturb me especially that they are being crowded out by budget cuts and "back to basics" courses. Indeed, the so-called basics are necessary and must get first priority, but after that there should be room for materials that can provide both teachers and students with accurate, realistic information on the present as well as on the long-range outlook.

It is essential that the level of debate be raised before any meaningful discussion of substantive issues can take place. For schoolchildren, many years of uncertainty and opportunity lie ahead. The process of identifying options and alternatives should be one of judgment based on the best information we can get. Blind optimism certainly is inappropriate preparation for the real world. But so is an unduly negative bias.

Schools aren't the only culprits promulgating this negative outlook. The media—television, newspapers, movies, and so on—reinforce the public perception of a coming "Dark Ages." While new technological and scientific breakthroughs are noted and briefly discussed, the caveats attached to their safety and effectiveness are dwelled upon at great length. For example, the virtual elimination of smallpox, diphtheria, and polio as fatal childhood illnesses is no longer newsworthy; instead, the news media emphasize an exaggerated nuclear threat to generations as yet unborn. Educators concerned about this pessimistic emphasis have little recourse to well-documented materials with a different viewpoint written for a nonspecialized adult audience. Few realistic (and therefore more optimistic) volumes exist.

Pointing out the dearth of recent, accurate, and balanced information is not to suggest the existence of some intentional, irresponsible educational conspiracy intent on depressing our children. Rather, the problem seems due partly to the difficulty of keeping current—a process of constantly revising, updating, and discarding classroom materials that no longer are timely. In a world of rapidly changing realities, the shelf life of texts on current events or social studies is not very long. The economics of publishing, unfortunately, work against the thoughtful revisions that often are needed. Already outdated, for instance, is the 1980 edition of Scott, Foresman's *The American Dream*. It covers population growth with two articles published in 1969, using population projections developed at the height of the postwar baby boom. Competent editors put these volumes together. But they failed to seek out qualified specialists with expertise in demographics, migration patterns, or fertility growth rates—or even to examine the information available from the United Nations Population Division, the United States Census Bureau, and many other qualified and readily accessible sources. Teachers, naturally enough, use the information available to them, even if it is inaccurate.

What, then, are the prospects for giving our children a more realistic and inspiring vision of the future? Pretty good, I think. In fact, we at The Hudson Institute have designed a program called Visions of the Future, the long-term objective of which is to provide teachers and students with the facts, theories, and analytical tools needed to evaluate the problems and challenges of their immediate and future environment. Specifically, the project has three aims:

1. To provide a realistic context in which to examine the inevitable (and, in many cases, currently unknown) problems of the United States as it moves from an industrial to a postindustrial society. Some costs and some pain will accompany the transition. Many new developments—including expanded production of synthetic materials, increased use of robots and automation, and further development of artificial intelligence—will have to be examined in terms of their potential for harm as well as for good. A realistic "futures" context can help identify and perhaps preempt some of these problems.
2. To be a "lobby for the future" and an "early warning net" that will raise our consciousness to the exciting prospects—and potential dangers—before us and to put both into a serious perspective. That is the principal reason behind this book.
3. To balance negative visions of the future based on misleading data or interpretations with more accurate forecasts based on the best, most recent information available.

This educational task is best approached through academic disciplines—economics, science, history, engineering, sociology, and political science. The Hudson Institute's appraisals of the current situation—as well as its projections of the future—are based on fairly persuasive factual evidence. But even those who remain skeptical cannot deny the validity of our effort to establish a more balanced perspective.

One of the great advantages of the Visions of the Future project is that the principle of providing accurate, documented, timely information can be applied to many subject areas. The critical variable is the enthusiasm and knowledge of the educator. We believe many teachers, administrators, and board members perceive the need to revise much of the course content dealing with recent events, to update facts and theories about where the world is heading, and to provide an antidote to the misleading claims that abound. Our program, therefore, primarily is concerned with curriculum development, to help teachers convey the latest information about their disciplines.

It is time to update the excessively pessimistic world view in vogue for the past decade. In addition to being counterproductive to the development of the kinds of citizens who take pride in their country, culture, and heritage, this negative outlook also is objectively unjustified. No one should be guaranteeing our children instant happiness or a trouble-free future, but we should be offering them at least the possibility of happiness and the near certainty of a future. Unfortunately, our textbooks usually don't do either one.

Herman Kahn

Prologue

Are we lying to our children? The question is laden with value judgments, assumptions, and emotions, but I think the answer is "Yes." This contemporary lie is an effort to underestimate and sometimes undermine what this nation has accomplished. One finds in many of our textbooks statements that imply an almost institutionalized misunderstanding of environmental problems and the plight of the poor. Rarely is the claim made—as it should be—that American economic development has in many ways had a positive impact on the development of less fortunate nations. Certainly problems accompany that development, but those problems don't detract from the American achievement.

Many texts convey the impression that material gains should be possible without risks or compromises or that the risks are not worth taking regardless of the potential benefits. Surely one would prefer development without any pollution, and certainly not all improvements in the standard of living justify even minimal contamination of the water supply. But any reasonable person must recognize the trade-offs in these calculations. Improvements usually come at a price. We may choose not to pay it, but we should understand that there are equally significant consequences for inaction. If I am not willing to pay the fuel bill or accept the energy use that accompanies air conditioning, then I shouldn't expect to cool my apartment during the hot summer months.

Analyses of costs and benefits rarely are considered in the textbooks. Instead one senses a naïve "all or nothing" calculation. Although this kind of formulation is not an outright lie, it does mislead. And that is precisely what concerns me.

Too often we are interested in simple solutions to complex questions. If the Hudson River is dirty, the response is "Clean it up." What the respondent doesn't consider is the price that must be paid to do the cleaning and whether those who will be affected—the taxpayers—are willing to pay it. Admittedly it is difficult to describe the complexity of some problems, but trade-offs are so much part of our lives that every child understands the concept intuitively.

Then there are those who simply take what we have for granted. In one textbook, for example, the authors discuss the "tragedy" of traffic jams. For someone who has lived through many of them it can seem enormously frustrating but hardly a tragedy. What the authors don't mention is the state of economic development and the mass distribution of goods that allow a society to have so many consumer products. They neglect to mention the freedom and mobility that automobiles provide, the ease with which one can go to the grocery or the seashore. They don't point out how difficult it was to travel a century ago—for example, the hazards of traveling over land routes before paved roads. Only one side of an evolutionary picture is presented—an unbalanced, negative view of a modern phenomenon. In not one recent textbook is there a comparative analysis of transportation in the nineteenth and the twentieth centuries. At the very least one would assume that an appreciation of historical conditions would inform a student's judgment about the present. Instead, the authors' bias dominates the perspective.

Related to this issue is the guilt many people feel about their own wealth as well as that of the nation. In Kenneth Keniston's *Young Radicals* a student is quoted as having said, "You don't know what hell is like till you've lived in Scarsdale." Since most people in America aspire to that "hell," you've got to wonder what guilt this young man must feel to inspire that statement. Although this exact quote isn't found in other textbooks, the general sentiment is.

It is often alleged that Americans use more than their fair share of resources. This argument is based on the supposition that a nation with 6 percent of the world's people should use 6 percent of the world's resources. Ignored in this equation is the fact that this nation produces 35 percent of the world's wealth, which benefits not only Americans but many other nations as well. Nor is it reasonable to penalize a nation for its productivity. The seemingly disproportionate use of resources can be regarded as a blessing if it enables us to produce what our people and other people want.

Whether or not it is a blessing, however, should not negate the fact that the assumption about population and resources was employed to make judgments; there was no mention of an equally plausible assumption about production and resources. In my opinion the first assumption is predicated on feelings of guilt and may elicit those feelings from students; the second suggests something about the distinctive characteristics of Americans and may elicit pride.

Another manifestation of this problem can be found in the "small is beautiful" argument, or what Kingsley Amis called the "more is worse" attitude. E. F. Schumacher has created the impression that the expansion of our industry and technology necessarily has an adverse effect on the society. Although there is a price one pays for technology, as I've suggested, there clearly are significant benefits. The issue that should be addressed is not whether small is beautiful or large is not, but whether the benefits justify the risks. Some extremists maintain that any risk is unacceptable. They argue that any man-made innovation that upsets the balance in nature is a risk worth avoiding. The phrase "balance in nature," however, also conceals many value judgments. Is one upsetting a natural balance by cutting down a tree or damming a river? Is every human intervention a violation of this balance?

Still another explanation is the Third World rhetoric that now predominates in the United Nations. Taking their lead from Olaf Palme and Willy Brandt, many nations have argued on the floor of the General Assembly that the industrialized countries have an "obligation" to assist the poor all over the world. Undoubtedly one can make this argument from a humanitarian point of view. One can even argue that self-interest dictates such action. But what should be included in the discussion is the view that inappropriate aid also can undermine the conditions necessary for production. If all it took were money, then poverty and famine would have been eliminated a long time ago. Yet the complexity of the "aid to the Third World" argument seems to elude some textbook writers who often accept political rhetoric as reality.

One recent development is the work of academics who use computer models and analyses to give us scenarios of the future. Surely computers are useful tools of analysis, however dependent on the quality of the information they are given. In any analysis, assumptions are critical. Therefore, if a programmer believes that the depletion of some minerals cannot be compensated for, it is logical to accept a disaster scenario as the outcome. If the programmer believes that man is not an adaptable creature but one who will continue certain practices even if they have negative effects, then it is sensible to conclude that a catastrophe will occur.

In both the Club of Rome report (1972)* and *The Global 2000 Report*, (1980),** these assumptions are made. It is revealing that both reports use the phrase "if present trends continue. . . ." They neglect to point out that trends don't always continue. Trends continue if they are going well or if you believe there are no alternatives or if you accept a very limited view of human adaptability. If certain trends were to have continued, the Great Lakes might now be an open sewer. Instead, pollution-producing activities were curtailed, and the lakes are cleaner today than at any time in the past thirty years. Similarly, if humans were not adaptable, the difficulty in obtaining whale oil would have permanently inhibited economic development. But that didn't happen because alternative sources of fuel were found. In short, even "scientific" models are only as accurate as their assumptions.

It seems to me that a balanced view of conditions usually is not reported in textbooks. For the moment at least, ecological doomsayers rule the cultural roost. One can't go to a cocktail party without hearing about some catastrophe. Television news programming usually creates the illusion that the world is coming to an end. The genre of disaster movies—for example, *China Syndrome* and *War Games*—is very popular. Many successful books have titles with the words "crisis," "doom," and "end."

The problem I have with this is that it is one thing to misinform adults on the 11-o'clock news but quite another to mislead youths under the guise of "education." How can most students possibly distinguish between fact and fiction in their high school social studies textbooks? Why should our students be misled?

---

*Club of Rome. Organization designed to help people understand linkage of global problems and responsibility of nations in solving these problems. Founded in Rome by Aurelio Peccei in 1968.

**The Global 2000 Report. Report organized for President Carter in 1980 that deals with environmental trends and their influence on the future of the globe.

Surely some social studies textbooks are better than others. But this book is not so much an attempt to evaluate the relative merits of textbooks as it is an effort to point out the misleading arguments that appear in all of them. What is examined, therefore, are the textbooks published in the past five years—presumably those that are the most up-to-date. None has been omitted from my critical examination, and all—it seems to me—have areas of imbalance or misleading arguments.

What I aim to emphasize is the faddist and "trendy" character of these books, which adopt the mood of the times without any concession to historical perspective. If this is the "era of limits," it might be recalled that a scant 20 years ago the "era of unlimited horizons" was in fashion. Has our society changed so quickly? Or was one claim a gross exaggeration and the other based on undue pessimism? Is historical reality somewhere between our wishes and our nightmare?

This book may upset some people. I hope it does. I make no bones about my desire to slay the faddist dragon of doom. In the process I hope that educators will reexamine what they are teaching and what they ought to be teaching. If that happens, I will have achieved my aim.

WHY ARE THEY LYING TO OUR CHILDREN?

1

Introduction

Oone evening more than a year ago I came home from the university to find my elder daughter—then 13—with tears streaming down her cheeks. Since this wasn't the first time I had encountered such a scene, my immediate reaction was to attribute this emotional outburst to a problem with her friends. Problems with friends like mood swings, are not unusual for a budding adolescent. This time, however, was different. When I gently inquired why she was crying, Staci said, "Because I don't have a future."

There are things my daughter doesn't have—for example, a father who lets her do pretty much what she wants—but her future, like that of most healthy, middle-class American children lucky enough to have parents who take parenting seriously, seems promising. To counter my assurances, Staci produced a mimeographed sheet suggesting that a dismal future—or none at all—is what awaits her. It detailed in vivid language the horrors of the next twenty-five years: worldwide famine; overpopulation (between eight billion and 10 billion people across the globe); air pollution so bad everyone will wear gas masks; befouled rivers and streams that will mandate cleansing tablets in our drinking water; a greenhouse effect that will account for the melting of the polar ice caps and worldwide devastation of coastal cities; and an epidemic of cancer brought on by damage to the ozone layer. At no point did the author of those claims mention probability, nor did words such as "might" or "unlikely" find their way into the text.

It was, by any standard, a litany of doom, and my daughter was certainly justified in grieving. The only problem, of course, is that the sheet's claims were misguided and misleading. What she read as a scenario for her future has about as much truth to it as the claim that kissing a frog will turn him into a prince. Perhaps less, since I've never kissed a frog and only can guess I

31

won't turn him into a prince. But I know that the earth Staci will inherit is in far better shape than that handout alleges. I kept asking myself why a teacher at a respectable private school in New York would try to frighten her students in this way. Moreover, why would these unsubstantiated claims be presented as factual evidence?

This was Act One in my unfolding drama. Act Two started several weeks later. My younger daughter sat down at the dinner table one evening and announced that by eating "so much" food we are depriving Cambodians (don't ask me why only Cambodians) of nutrition. Nancy's teacher had explained that because there is a finite world food supply, our "overeating" led to deprivation for others. This was a thematic variation on my mother's old line: "You should know how lucky you are to have those peas; after all, there are people starving in Europe." I could never figure out what relationship my eating peas had to starving children in Europe. In fact, I would have been overjoyed to let them have all my peas.

Now I faced a new wrinkle. My daughter was convinced by her teacher in another reputable private school that by eating "too much" she was taking food out of the mouths of starving children. I was curious to know what "too much" might be and how Nancy's newly discovered self-control would affect the starving children of Cambodia. When I asked these questions my 10-year-old said, "Well I don't know, but my teacher does."

The curtain rose on Act Three. I decided to find out why teachers in schools that charge as much annual tuition as I pay for a new Chevy can be so utterly out of touch with reality and so cavalier toward the emotional sensitivities of my kids. In the first instance I discovered the teacher of my older daughter was charming and well-meaning. Her sheet of future despair was prompted by her own uncritical reading of the student text.

When I told her that the events she depicted are not likely to occur, she replied, "How do you know?" Desperately trying to be polite, I pointed out with all the equanimity I could muster that Chicken Little also predicted that the sky was falling but as far as I could tell it was still up there. Doomsayers have long predicted the end is near, but I don't see many sane people preparing for it. At some point far in the future the catastrophists may turn out to be right, but it is unreasonable and unproductive to accept these arguments for the foreseeable future. Her answer—which one might expect—was "It's all in the book."

I now moved on to the other private school that affects my life at home. The teacher of my younger daughter is not so charming and well-meaning. She is from the "I know what's best for your child" school of thought. I politely asked if she tells her class, "Eating too much food here accounts for starvation in Cambodia." She said, "Yes, I do say that. It's a good moral lesson for my students." "But what"—I couldn't help saying—"if it isn't true? If I eat half a turkey breast instead of a whole breast, is the other part put in cellophane wrap and sent to a starving child in Cambodia? Will my doggie bag of leftovers end up as a CARE package?" I saw the combination of anger and recognition in her eyes. "You've got a point, Mr. London. But we do eat too much and others have too little. Isn't that true?" I could tell there was little sense in pursuing the point. The curtain closed on Act Three.

This little drama is not a story unique to my family. Fire-and-brimstone logic is combined with fear-and-doomsday psychology in educational materials across the country. What I experienced could be retold tens of thousands of times, about children in public and private schools, in high schools and at elementary levels, with conservative and with liberal teachers, in wealthy neighborhoods and poor. A tidal wave of pessimism has swept across the country, leaving in its wake grief, despair, immobility, and paralysis. Gresham's law of education today seems to be that bad news—even when false—will drive good news out of circulation.

Why, it might be asked, should this be the case? Most Americans live better than their parents; most parents, far better than their children's grandparents. Any dispassionate comparison of life in America circa 1983 and 1883 would suggest things are better now in almost every conceivable way than they were then. Yet if I were to say, as Dr. Pangloss once did, "This is the best of all possible worlds," I would be considered a pessimist rather than a pollyannaish optimist. Most young people would argue, "You mean this is the best we can do? Ugh!" This condition is partially a function of the "the more you have the less you appreciate" attitude. But that is not a sufficient explanation.

The attitude that prevails in our schools is the result of media speculation on the fate of the environment, textbook material that largely or in part conveys pessimistic impressions, and audiovisual material that often was produced according to doomsday scenarios.

To give you some idea of the excesses to which producers of educational materials have gone, let me cite one egregious example. In 1971 the Canadian Film Board produced a six-minute educational film entitled *Paradise Lost*. It is shown in grades two through six to awaken interest in environmental questions. There isn't any narration to accompany the filmstrip; students usually are asked to draw their own conclusions. The film begins with an unidentified airplane dropping gaseous material onto a marvelously bucolic scene in a forest. The children might consider the plane to be a crop duster, although it resembles a conventional jet transport. The birds and butterflies that had formerly been flying about freely in an ambiance right out of *Bambi* attempt to escape from the noxious gases. But wherever they fly, the fumes engulf them. Finally the birds keel over, and butterflies fall on top of them. The wind blows fallen leaves over the birds and butterflies, forming a symbolic gravesite as the words "The End" appear on the screen.

When I watched this film with a third-grade class, the teacher asked, "What do you think of the film?" One eight-year-old with a tear in the corner of her eye proclaimed, "I hate that airplane; it has no feeling for our friends in the forest." The teacher—quite satisfied with that response—sought additional replies. They were all similar. At no point did she ask, "How many of you have flown in an airplane? What are its advantages?" Or to take a different tack, "What is a crop duster and what does it do?" Instead the youngsters were given the gospel according to Rachel Carson. Airplanes and, by implication, technology are enemies of forest creatures and their two-legged protectors.

What can one possibly conclude from this? For the uninitiated, in this case the schoolchildren, the conclusion is that our friends in nature are the innocent victims of mankind's insensitivity. This is an alarmist, unbalanced, contentious, propagandistic, and unfair viewpoint. Yet in many respects it reflects the textbook material it supplements.

At the end of the film *Annie Hall*, Woody Allen says that his philosophy of life was developed when his mother—on one of the family sojourns to a Catskills resort—would argue, "The food is awful, just terrible, and the portions are so small." So it is with the conception of modern technology. It has some disadvantages and doesn't always produce miracles. But the miracles it does produce are taken for granted. Children know what a plane can do, how it has shortened distance, held back the hands of time, given people wings, taken us to Grandma in Florida, and brought us adventures unimagined by our nineteenth-century ancestors.

In 1972, when the Club of Rome report *Limits to Growth* by Dennis and Dana Meadows et al. was published, the argument for disaster had reached the height of seemingly scientific validation. A research team concluded that if resources continue to be used at the current rate, the world will run out of food, be overrun with population and pollution, face a widening gap of rich and poor, and confront technology that is hazardous to our health and safety. To use the language of the report:

> If present trends in world population, industrialization, pollution, food production, and resource depletion continue unchanged, the limits to growth on this planet will be reached sometime within the next 100 years.
>
> The most probable result will be a rather sudden and uncontrollable decline in both population and industrial capacity.

This report had a profound effect on the national psyche. While serious scholars denounced the research methodology and its conclusions, the book's influence on public opinion was notable. It, along with *Small Is Beautiful*, sounded the alarm for imminent catastrophe unless we mend our ways and devise methods for living in harmony with nature.

It is worth noting that two years after its report the Club of Rome modified its findings, significantly recanting the earlier statements and calling them an "overreaction." Ten years later the principal author, Dennis Meadows, admitted that one of the things he would change from his 1972 study is to "tell the people that the power to change lies with them." Although this may not seem like much of an admission, it dramatically alters what was done earlier. After all, *Limits to Growth* was a result of mathematical modeling that intentionally relied on the continuation of then present trends; human intervention, on the other hand, presupposes no such inevitability. In fact, it is precisely such human intervention that makes all trends unreliable. The late René Dubos, in an interview with Bill Moyers, contended:

> Present trends never continue. . . . If there is something about human beings it is that they never stand idle in front of a situation that threatens them provided they can see the consequences of it. They start doing something about it.

But in the early 1970s the Club of Rome report reinforced sentiments of fear, guilt, and shame that are still with us in educational textbooks and teacher instructional materials.

Many supporters of this point of view maintain that even if the arguments are wrong, the sentiments are right. Presumably they feel that the fear of shortages will encourage public support for desirable policies—for example, conservation. But frightening people into "good" policies does not necessarily ensure the desired results. By suggesting the inevitability of disaster one also can promote a "live for today, the hell with tomorrow" attitude, which is the antithesis of what they want.

When previous generations of Americans learned about the triumph of American ingenuity and production, it gave them a sense of accomplishment and pride. Today, however, with technology often viewed as a menace, our children are taught that U.S. economic production is the cause of global problems and that this nation's technical and scientific ingenuity is a source of human woe. With this world view, it is hard not to believe that America's role in history is malevolent. Is it any wonder that patriotism often is used in a pejorative sense and that many young Americans are unwilling to defend national interests? Is it any wonder that the past is not viewed as a guide to the present, that our moral standing is condemned by the young, that our national goals are obscure, and that the belief in the future—the linchpin of our democracy—has seriously eroded?

In 1980 the National Education Association published a guide for teachers of future studies that was prepared by Draper Kauffman and titled *Futurism and Future Studies*. Among other things, this document makes the following astonishing claims:

> Food production is losing the race with the population explosion, and a massive famine within the decade seems probable. The main question remaining is whether famine will come in a single global disaster, or whether it will come as a chronic series of regional famines.
> The earth lacks the resources and the pollution-absorbing capacity which would be needed to support a situation in which all nations are developed to the economic level of Western Europe. Thus, economic development is likely to prove a false hope to many of the poorest fourth of the world's peoples. . . .
> Every elimination of a habitat or species, every introduction of a new artificial chemical, and every increase in the demand we are already making on the environment represents an increased risk of unknowingly crossing some threshold which will cause the system to collapse.
> A shift to . . . slow-to-no growth [is] likely for the economy as a whole. Although no-growth might be desirable for many non-economic reasons, it would give the developing nations

among them the opportunity to catch up, it poses a serious threat to the economic stability of all industrialized nations.

Nowhere in this so-called guidebook is there the slightest reference to the constructive role of wealthy nations in the global economy; to the rapid economic growth that has propelled many non-Western nations into the middle-income ranks; to the general record of declining resource prices and the reasons for it; to the reduction of air pollution in our major cities and the immensely successful program to clean our rivers and streams that has already borne dramatic results in the Great Lakes. What we have in Kauffman's guide is a return to the concept of "Spaceship Earth" that depicts a limited universe with static resources and dwindling supplies that a few greedy bullies will gobble up to the detriment of the Earth's poor. There is no suggestion that the percentage of the world's poor has declined significantly in this century, or that "resources" encompass ingenuity, technology, and labor, not simply the minerals in the ground.

Henry James once described unhappiness as a "disease." In our time it has reached epidemic proportions, and Typhoid Mary appears to us in cinematic entertainment, the late news, and teacher guidebooks. Predictions of doom have always been with us. The nostrums of Nostradamus and the prophecies of Cassandra have something in common: a belief that gloom, if not doom, is on the horizon. What distinguishes this era from others, however, is that gloom is now presented as a series of scientific verities, not as mere speculation.

It is curious that a mere 20 years ago pedagogy emphasized relativism. Theoretically, the presentation of two opposing points of view was more desirable than having only one viewpoint considered. But since most students didn't have the slightest idea of the intellectual edifice supporting either of the arguments, the option of any choice was absurd. It was a little like asking a typical New Yorker if he prefers speaking Urdu or Uzbek.

But the present educational establishment doesn't even pretend to offer options. Instead, in the name of survival it offers preachments that are essentially a package of New Testament virtues and preindustrial simplicity. Whether presented as a means to avert doomsday or, more moderately, as a way to adapt to an austere future, nearly all of the "new" themes are traditional: a rejection of crass materialism, responsibility for the less fortunate (the modern equivalent of the "white man's burden" and the "waste not, want not" principle), harmony with nature, cooperation instead of competition. The only truly novel ingredient is the *ethical* importance of limiting fertility.

From a pedagogical viewpoint the relativism of the past has been exchanged for the theology of the 1980s. What educational philosophers such as John Dewey argued against—a pedagogy based on fear and guilt—has been restored as neo-Puritanism. What makes this exercise so ironic is that educators throughout most of this century conceived of child development in Pelagian (human beings are essentially good) rather than Augustinian (human beings are conceived in sin and must be forced to do right) terms. It was the teacher's task to cultivate and nurture the child's intrinsic natural goodness. This mission was embedded in Enlightenment thoughts and most vividly described in Rousseau's *Émile*, which to some degree anticipated the twentieth-century as "the era of the child."

Now, however, education in general and future studies in particular depict man as fraught wtih original sin. It probably is not coincidental that less than 15 years after it was fashionable to romanticize youth (achieved through the glorification of the counterculture), there is an effort to shame children into being "virtuous" and narrowly doctrinaire about the future. The unfolding of this attitudinal change can be discovered in textbooks and teacher guides that elevate moral instruction above adherence to the canons of scholarship. John D. Haas in *Future Studies in the K-12 Curriculum* (a teacher guide sponsored by the National Institute of Education) makes precisely this point most graphically:

> . . . I tend to agree with those futurists who see the need to abandon (or at least to modify) those values and assumptions of Western industrialization that have brought these societies to the brink of disaster and that threaten the future existence of our species.

For almost two centuries it has been fashionable for artists and literary figures to denounce technological advances as "a tyranny of body and mind." But this view has been almost exclusively restricted to intellectuals. Blake's famous line "these dark satanic mills" was a classic nineteenth-century intellectual's rendering of the factory system. By any fair evaluation, however, the factory system—even with its many hateful flaws—represented a considerable improvement in the life of the average person. Romantic literature and art may have condemned the machine and exalted rural life, but for the average person who experienced the untold hardship and oppression of preindustrial society, literature was dismissed to the dustbin of history.

Early factories were certainly harsh and dismal places to work in; yet those man-made cruelties, however severe, could not compare to the difficulties of eking out a livelihood on the farms. When Coleridge, Disraeli, and Carlyle, among others, criticized the factories, they did so without any regard for the people who enjoyed the benefits of longer lives, better food, and better housing than their forefathers, notwithstanding the many exceptions to the rule. Carlyle made the "machine" the symbol of the society he deplored, and nineteenth-century poets invariably represented fires in iron foundries as the cauldron of hell. For them material progress was accompanied by a breakdown in spiritual values. This is also, of course, the argument of many twentieth-century environmentalists.

The intellectual of the nineteenth and twentieth centuries, especially in his role as literary spokesman, was and still is preoccupied with beauty and simplicity. This explains in part why—with very few exceptions—novelists are naturalists. But there exists a yawning gulf between the intellectual and the world's economic realities (although the successful writer is aware of the fact that his royalty checks are due to the economic prosperity he is so glib in denouncing). The intellectual usually scoffs at financial enhancement and thrives instead on "malaise," sanctified in his mission by what Lionel Trilling called "the adversary culture." The intellectual is the disturber of the peace, a rebel against creature comforts and technological advances.

One of these intellectual spokesmen, Dr. Bernard Dixon, expresses the extreme view that the environment must remain unchanged. In an article in *New Scientist* (1976), he argues:

Some of us who might happily bid farewell to a virulent virus or bacterium may well have qualms about eradicating forever a "higher" animal—whether rat or bird or flea—that passes on such microbes to man. . . . Where, moving up the size and nastiness scale (smallpox virus, typhoid fever bacilli, malarial parasites, schistosomiosis worms, locusts, rats . . .), does conservation become important? There is, in fact, no logical line that can be drawn. Every one of the arguments adduced by conservationists applies to the world of vermin and pathogenic microbes just as they apply to whales, gentians and flamingoes. Even the tiniest and most virulent virus qualifies.

This argument suggests that every creation, every microbe on God's Earth, has some purpose—sometimes hidden to us—that cannot be disturbed without significant harm to the future of the globe. Any technological change, however minor, is believed to modify the relationship of man to his environment and as a consequence uproot the essential balance in nature. If Prometheus is unbound, Dr. Dixon would have him pinned and tethered.

David Ehrenfeld, a professor at Rutgers University, writes in *The Arrogance of Humanism*, "Most scientific discoveries and technological inventions can be developed in such a way that they are capable of doing great damage to human beings, their culture, and their environments." Certainly any reasonable person would admit that science and technology can do great damage and have been responsible for environmental damage, but it is equally true that science has improved the material conditions of mankind, eliminated many of mankind's most dread diseases, and invited romantic visions heretofore considered beyond our imagination.

The idea of an ecology so fragile that it is unable to cope with human interference does not square with a global history that includes an ice age, flooding, worldwide pestilence, and every plague God could conceive of to impose on Pharaoh's Egypt. But a world in which mankind does not tamper with nature is a world in which insects, animals, and microbes declare war on their two-legged neighbors. Nature uncontrolled is not benign. What would be the price of an unspoiled wilderness? Aside from the millions of deaths caused by the diseases scientific advances have eliminated, the explosion in the insect population would be incalculable. The view of mankind as Tarzan or Robinson Crusoe is a marvelous literary metaphor but an impractical guide to human behavior.

For the antiscience and antitechnology advocates, the human spirit is static, frozen in time. Pleasures are or should be simple and our environment pristine. The only problem with this depiction is that human beings have a continual urge to improve their condition. To transcend the plight of animals subject to nature's whim has always been a human characteristic. It seems to me worth asking why, if God wanted the world unchanged, did He give people the power to think.

Robert Pirsig in his book *Zen and the Art of Motorcycle Maintenance* makes this argument:

> He [man] had built empires of scientific capability to manipulate the phenomena of nature into enormous manifestations of his own dreams of power and wealth—but for this he had exchanged an empire of understanding of equal magnitude: an understanding of what it is to be a part of the world, and not an enemy of it.

What, precisely, is being "a part of the world"? To Pirsig it is a transcendental feeling of harmony with nature combined with reason to create tranquillity. However, nature isn't essentially tranquil; it is erratic and often violent. The idea of being part of the world generally includes some form of struggle with nature. Am I part of the world or an enemy of it when I step on a blade of grass? Am I an enemy of the environment when I ride in my car instead of walking? Is Jonas Salk an enemy of nature for finding a cure for polio?

For some people, any manifestation of nature—from animal to microbe—should be conserved because it exists and because this existence is a stage of an historical and majestic evolutionary process. Surely there is some validity to this claim—but only some. Is it not true that mankind's condition is evolving from one in which most people were impoverished to one in which most will be well off? As animals use nature for the survival of their species, so must man. Admittedly humans can and do treat nature capriciously. Mine is not a defense of those who litter or kill animals for the sheer pleasure of it. But I do not see the utility or good sense in ignoring man's unique role in nature and the history of natural adaptation to changing conditions.

C. D. Stone, scholar and lawyer, in a book entitled *Should Trees Have Standing?*, presents the case for the legal rights of forests, a position based on the view that forests should not be affected by human inadvertence. But what Stone ignores is that mankind can and does plant as well as cut down. He uses the fruits of nature and replenishes those fruits, sometimes improving the conditions he finds. Those trees can be used to improve the conditions of mankind, other animals, and much of the natural environment. Should we guarantee the rights of trees against lumberjacks? And if we do that for trees, why not streams, blades of grass, and even microbes? At what point does the legal protection of nature adversely affect mankind?

Charles Elton in *The Ecology of Invasions by Animals and Plants* proposes several reasons for conservation, including "because it is a right relation between man and living things, because it gives opportunities for richer experience. . . ." However, Elton doesn't tell us what "the right relation" is, nor is "richer experience" as he observes it a widely accepted view.

Coexistence can take many forms, including, I might add, a role for people in altering the natural setting for the benefit of nature and occasionally for the selfish benefit of mankind. It is also true that camping in a natural setting can be a very enriching experience. But that is generally because we can return to a warm room and a shower when the experience is over. Is it a rich experience to consider your camp your home? Is it a rich experience to be caught in a flood tide without a means of escape? Is being attacked by a shark the "right relation" with living things?

Admittedly many areas of life man has tried to harness have not yielded to his will. But it would require a very distorted imagination to ignore the very effective control we have established to reduce the high rates of infant mortality, bleak labor conditions, and the oppressive poverty of a scant 50 years ago. In some respects the world has not improved, but in most respects it has. And this improvement has been brought about by the human desire to shape the character of the environment.

Faulkner cautioned in *Go Down Moses,*

> that doomed wilderness whose edges were being constantly and punily gnawed at by men with plows and axes who feared it because it was wilderness.

Yet those same men overcame that fear to build temples of stone that reached the sky and let their spirits soar. Only an author living in twentieth-century affluence could so eloquently mourn the loss of wilderness. Yet Faulkner was on to something. He was wrestling wtih mankind's fundamental nature. Is our nature to reach an accommodation with those around us, to restore our relationship with the environment to one of "harmony," or is our spirit unbounded, filled with promise to improve our conditions?

Some people, including many textbook authors, view life as limitation. For them God's plan is not subject to alteration; science is the enemy of Providence. They view a land defiled as the result of "progress," and that price is unbearable. But what these advocates ignore is that this is the first generation in recorded time so to enjoy the fruits of technological innovation that a concern with nature is now feasible. The wilderness is appreciated because of our air-conditioned and insect-free homes and a transportation system that conveniently brings us to and returns us from its hostile fringes.

This evolutionary heritage must be preserved. But how much of it? At what price? Is conservation more important than the elimination of poverty? Do we subscribe to a standard of living that brings us closer to nature and closer to our animal instincts? Do we maintain nature's primordial condition, or do we change it to improve our lives? To see no difference between man and natural conditions is absurd and ultimately immoral. Nature neither thinks nor feels pain. It seems to me that if the choice must be made between mankind and nature, I am in the corner of my fellow humans, albeit the choice itself is a reflection of the impending-disaster scenarios of those who are convinced our tinkering with the environment will result in catastrophe.

As Eric Hoffer pointed out, "Faith in a holy cause is to a considerable extent a substitute for the lost faith in ourselves." Some environmentalists obviously have turned their backs on humanism. They see man in nature as Dr. Frankenstein's monster. Having decoded the secrets of science, Frankenstein loses control over his own creation. In this story technology is the problem because once it has been unleashed it presumably can't be controlled. Mary Shelley's nightmare has been imposed on a generation of youngsters familiar with stories of technologically induced horrors. It is as if science is synonymous with horror.

In *2001: A Space Odyssey,* Stanley Kubrick has a computer, H.A.L., mutiny against the captain of the spaceship. Although this is typical science-fiction material, it also is related to the belief that technology cannot be controlled, that once the genie is out of the bottle, human intervention can't be restored.

This fear is reinforced by the television news depiction of many current events. The Three Mile Island "disaster," for example, was a much-exaggerated description of a serious accident. According to the news reports, thousands of Harrisburg residents were threatened by an "imminent meltdown" and by the radiation vented into the atmosphere. In retrospect we know there were no casualties. We also know that despite many unanticipated errors in judgment, the condition of the nuclear plant was nowhere near meltdown. And we know that the level of radiation released during the height of this "man-made crisis" was lower than the routine daily expiration of radiation from Dutch and French nuclear energy reactors.

With a fear of technology rather pervasive in our news reporting, with some environmentalists encouraging the belief that we have no right to tamper with nature, with literary figures from two centuries cataloguing the horrible conditions brought about by technology, with scientists using models based on inaccurate assumptions to predict future gloom and perhaps doom, it is little wonder that teachers and textbook writers often cannot distinguish between wheat and chaff. As a result, they become part of a system that disseminates the currently popular, prevailing opinions. Unfortunately, those opinions tend to be wrong, misleading, and misguided.

2

Population and Food

Because of the law of diminishing returns, food tends not to keep up with the geometric progression rate of growth of population.

Thomas Malthus, *Essay on the Principle of Population* **(1798)**

F ew ideas have so systematically penetrated the public imagination as Thomas Malthus' notion of population growth. His idea is simple and logically persuasive. Malthus argued that as population increases, the relative size of the globe (livable and farmable space) decreases until it has shrunk so substantially that food supplies fall below the level necessary for life. Behind this argument is the belief that mouths to feed will surpass hands to cultivate the land. This position is compelling because it *seems* logical and because stories of famine and starvation in overpopulated regions in the past 30 years appear to reinforce its accuracy. However, both the logic and the accuracy can easily be disproved.

For one thing, neither of the assumptions about population and food production is correct. Nothing in our history suggests there is anything inevitable about population outstripping food supplies, yet that is precisely what one reads in many social studies textbooks. Scott, Foresman's *People on Earth* (1983) includes the claim that "world population has been doubling nearly every thirty-five years." That claim is based on a set of very misleading Malthusian assumptions about the geometric rate of population growth. From the beginning of recorded history until about 1776, population growth was static. Only from the late eighteenth-century until the mid-1960s was it on a steadily upward slope; since 1965 the rate of growth has been declining at a substantial rate. For example, world population growth was 2.1 percent in 1965 and 1.7 percent in 1981.

The only way in which these textbook claims can be supported is to analyze population growth very selectively and then to project trends on the basis of this narrow perspective. If I were to apply this reasoning to my adolescent daughters, who have been growing at the rate of two inches a year, it would mean that they will dwarf Wilt Chamberlain by the time they are 25. However, before I rush them into professional basketball contracts, I should consider the obvious: They will not grow at two inches a year much longer, and the likelihood is they will not be taller than six feet.

Many textbooks rely on the peak of the baby boom to make projections about population at the end of the century. What they invariably neglect to say is that this is a "peak" in an unprecedented boom. It is curious that books published long after the decrease in population growth commenced continue to predict geometric increases in population and arithmetic increases in food production. Follett's *World Geography* (1983) states that population will inevitably outstrip "the rate at which farmers are able to increase food production." To support this contention, a footnote in the teacher's edition points out:

In the early 1960s, according to most estimates, the world had a 95 day supply of grain reserves. By the mid-1970's the grain reserve had been reduced to a 26-day supply. Disaster relief, poor harvest due to unseasonable weather, and increases in population growth accounted for much of the reduction.

What the author of this book doesn't point out is that the grain reserves are not especially significant as an indicator of nutrition levels; much more relevant is information about actual consumption. Moreover, disasters and unseasonable weather are not regular occurrences on which to base harvest estimates. If the scenario developed here were a true description of the relationship between population and food supply, more people and less food would mean higher food prices. Yet that is not the global pattern.

Consumption of food per person throughout the world has been increasing over the past 30 years. Moreover, no data indicate that the bottom-income quartile is faring worse than before, or that it hasn't shared in the general improvement of nutritional conditions. Africa is the one continent where food production per capita has not kept pace with this general description, but most experts agree this is attributable almost entirely to government policies and social conditions, not to any kind of "inevitable" global trends. Deaths through famine have decreased in the past century in relative as well as in absolute terms. World food prices have been trending downward for decades, even centuries, and there is good reason to believe this trend will persist. The price of wheat relative to wages has been declining since 1800. And although the pattern is not as consistent, the price of wheat relative to the consumer price index has also declined since 1800. World grain and food production per person from 1950 to 1982 shows a continuous increase. Similarly, corn yields from 1930 to 1979 demonstrate a straight-upward-sloping trend line.

The typical farmer in the United States understands the real problem: abundance. Food production is now so great and food stocks in the world so high that U.S. farmers are suffering economically. Agricultural yields per acre have continued to rise throughout most of this century, and this has been accomplished with a rapidly decreasing proportion of the labor force. Jean Mayer, a noted nutritionist, has written, "There is now widespread agreement that the availability of food per person is *greater today* [my emphasis] than twenty years ago." This, however, doesn't mean that every person on this globe has all the food he or she wants or that starvation doesn't exist. Many people who desperately need food don't have the money to buy it, and many countries that get food assistance don't distribute it to those in greatest need. As I've already suggested, uneven distribution of these supplies—whether due to incompetence or political or bureaucratic policies—often is a much more serious concern than food supply, even in a world with population increases. Nonetheless, some of our textbook writers choose to believe otherwise.

Macmillan's *Global Geography* (1981) text begins by postulating the potential for conflict due to too many people and too little food:

> Suppose you are a survivor of a shipwreck. . . . You find an island and are soon joined by several others. But you become alarmed when more people join your community. The more there are, the less food there is to go around. . . . Growing numbers of people are straining resources and leading to overpopulation. . . . It is hard to imagine the immensity of the problem.

Accordingly, the book goes on to describe a hypothetical family with four children in a less-developed country, each of whom has four children and they in turn each have four: ". . . All sixty-four human beings may have to make a living or feed themselves by using about the same amount of land that supported the original family of six individuals." It goes on, "Even in good crop years, ten to twenty million people in the world starve to death. Every night, about two-thirds of the world's people go to bed hungry. Yet in a little over 40 years, there will be twice as many people in the world to be fed."

This epitomizes the problem of doomsday logic: The first and most obvious flaw in the argument is that geometric population growth is inevitable. In fact, as income and education levels rise, birth rates fall, even when birth-control measures are not em-

54

ployed. The second flaw is the assumption that as this family grows, its members will all remain on the same parcel of land to eke out a living. The history of this century indicates that you need fewer farmers to produce more food than ever before. Technology has replaced hands, and less land is required to produce increasingly greater amounts of food. In 1900 more than 50 percent of the U.S. population was engaged in farming; today it is approximately 3 percent. And even with this decrease in labor, output has increased to the point where food is one of our major exports. This situation is not unique to the United States; it is essentially the same worldwide. But the miracles brought about by the Green Revolution by artificial methods of farming, hydroponics, artificial foods, and new fertilizers are not presented nearly as dramatically as the vision of Malthusian desperation.

The third flaw in the textual argument is the implication that starvation is related to the present rate of population growth and food supply. The number 10 million to 20 million starving each year (a formulation of U.N. statisticians whose experience is primarily with "have-not" countries) is not only excessive, it also ignores historical perspective. In 1969–70 an estimated third of Bengal's population of 30 million perished due to food shortages. In 1943 Indian casualties due to famine were four times greater than the total number of American and British civilians and soldiers who lost their lives in World War II. In the late 1950s China used food as a political weapon to deprive approximately a tenth of its total population (60 million people) of their rations. Starvation, in other words, has been a condition of life from the beginning of recorded history. This doesn't mean that we should accept it or turn our backs on it. But we should understand that it was even more prevalent before Parson Malthus formulated his theories in the nineteenth century than it has been at any time since then. And it is a condition that has steadily been alleviated despite droughts, natural disasters, and man-made problems.

The fourth flaw involves one of the great apocryphal statements of our time: "Every night, about two-thirds of the world's people go to bed hungry." This statement—which appears in a third of current social studies texts—is not accurate. In 1950 Lord Boyd-Orr, director general of the Food and Agriculture Organization, wrote in *Scientific American*: "A lifetime of malnutrition and actual hunger is the lot of at least two-thirds of mankind." This statement, based on the food distribution and drought problems in India and China, failed to mention the specific causes of these conditions or offer any historical perspective on the matter.

In 1973 a very reasonable book was published entitled *The Nutrition Factor* by Alan Berg of the Brookings Institute. In his last chapter Mr. Berg makes the following argument: "Without improved nutrition in the less-favored two-thirds of the world, the development of human resources—and the development of the nations themselves—may well be retarded." This is at least a statement of contingency—the words "without improved" and "may" suggest the possibility of preempting this possibility. However, to many less-careful readers this idea of retarded human and national development has become affirmation of a widely held belief, however contrary to the facts. In particular, hunger in China has been virtually eliminated, and in India great strides have been taken toward reducing starvation. Since India and China account for about half of the world's population, they are key players in any calculation that refers to "two-thirds" of the world's people.

Out-of-date statements as well as ones based on contingencies are easily found as the basis for declarative claims in textbooks, while counterclaims seem to be excluded systematically. For example, William Murdock, an expert on food production, wrote in an article in *Current* titled "World Food Hunger" (in the same year that Macmillan's *Global Geography* was published):

> Food production in virtually every poor country is great enough to provide an adequate diet for everyone. . . . More important, the poor nations could greatly increase their food production. . . . The notion that peasants are pushed onto marginal land . . . through "population pressures" is generally incorrect.

This kind of statement is not reprinted in our textbooks, nor is this documented point of view even considered. At this point the reader might ask, Why is there starvation at all if you allege there is enough food to go around? The principal reasons for starvation are man-made: wars that disrupt the pattern of food production; economic disincentives for farmers; poor distribution systems; and political corruption. There are also natural disasters that temporarily interfere with yields. But droughts and earthquakes do not last forever. The more typical pattern of food production and consumption suggests fewer deaths due to starvation and better nutrition due to increased food production worldwide. Yet the current social studies texts paint a very different picture, ignoring these realities altogether.

In the Silver Burdett *This Is Our World* (1981) teacher edition, the author recommends that instructors "Write on the chalkboard the following quotation, from Paul R. Ehrlich's book *Population Bomb* (1968): 'While you are reading these words, four people will have died of starvation. Most of them are children.'" The teacher is urged to have students compute annual starvation deaths on the basis of four per 30 seconds. Ehrlich predicted that in 15 years (1983), American harvests would decline precipitously to 25 million metric tons (the actual rate in 1982 was more than 75 million metric tons). As he put it, by that time steak will have become "a memory," the young will consume "special low mercury cod," and food rationing will have commenced. Nonetheless, one billion people will have starved to death during the 1970s and "population control laws . . . aimed at blacks and the poor" will have resulted after years of urban riots. It might be notes that Paul Ehrlich was and continues to be among the best-known and most influential of the "experts" writing on this subject.

Prentice-Hall's *The Future of the Environment* (1977) also suggests that our futures are probably grim, but at the same time notes that "forecasting probable futures is just the first step. Trends can be reversed or changed. And you can help change them." This acknowledgment of human intervention is a refreshing change in attitude, however short-lived. Several pages later in the same book there is an abridgment of a short story in which New York City has 35 million people by 1999 (more than a 600 percent increase in two decades) and people are rioting in the streets over soybean meat substitutes. Another "forecast," with the title "The Human Race Has Maybe Thirty-Five Years Left," is equally apocalyptic. Now, what can young persons possibly conclude after reading such articles in a textbook? Even if they are told that their generation can change the trends, how does this stand up against visions of rioting in the streets and "end of the world" prophecies? Students may be familiar with the notion that Americans "solve the difficult now and the impossible a little later," but there does not appear to be a "later" in these texts to worry about. In the Follet *World Geography* text mentioned earlier, a sheaf of grain is pitted against a skull and crossbones in an obvious competition between life and death. Death seemingly wins.

Laidlaw's *A History of Our American Republic* (1981) and several other texts cite Garret Hardin's argument that "every life saved this year in a poor country diminishes the quality of life for subsequent generations." Not only is this social Darwinism at its worst, it also is inaccurate, since it is based on the assumption that the population explosion has not been curtailed. Hardin gives little credit to the improvement in sanitary conditions, modern obstetrics, and medical techniques that have radically reduced infant deaths and increased life-spans; apparently he is uninterested in birth-control programs and improved standards of living that have already reduced population growth in the Third World.

What is most disturbing is the marshaling of "factual" errors to support conclusions of disaster and hopelessness. In Merrill's *Global Insights* (1980), for example, the section on India contains the statement that "149 Indian babies out of 1,000 die each year," followed by the claim that "between one-third and one-half of all babies die."

Nick Eberstadt of the Harvard Center for Population Studies maintains that less than one-quarter of the number estimated by the United Nations Food and Agriculture Organization to be "desperately hungry" are underfed. The true figure, he contends, is "a lower fraction, in all likelihood, than for any previous generation in man's recorded history." He bases this claim on several factors. First is the increase in food production and the generally improved means of distribution. Second is the stake that many less-developed nations have in exaggerating their problems to extract generous aid programs from the industrialized nations. And last, if desperate hunger were indeed as widespread as is often alleged, there would be less chance of survival and a contraction of life-expectancy rates. Instead we have life expectancy rising in both less-developed and more-developed nations. From 1950–55 to 1970–75, life expectancy rose from 42.6 to 53.4 years in the less-developed world (an even more substantial rise was evident in Asia). In the same time frame, the advanced nations experienced an increase in life expectancy from 65.2 to 71.2 years. However, these points are systematically excluded from textbooks.

There is also no explanation why the Ginn text *Exploring World Cultures,* which was published in 1981, uses a 1955 figure for Indian life expectancy—42 years—which is 11 years lower than the mid-1970s estimate. Or why another geography text, Globe's *The New Exploring of a Changing World* (1980), generalizes life expectancy in less-developed nations as "30 to 35 years" when that number was estimated to be 53 years in 1975. Follett's *Our World Today* (1983) includes the statement that "the population continues to grow faster and faster" and that "world population continues to grow at an increasingly rapid rate." A "J" curve graph shows 8 billion people in 2010 (another Follett book, *World Geography* [1983], shows 8 billion people in 2000).

The main point is that these assertions, as well as the statistical estimates, are far out of line with any population projections, including those overly pessimistic estimates at the United Nations. No recent text compares the difference between a population "J" curve (where the rate of growth continues to increase) and an "S" curve (which shows growth to have peaked and is on the decline)—a clear indication that theories of exponential growth still prevail and that the issue is not well understood by the textbook authors. As should be noted, the hump in a population "S" curve is related to the coming of age of the baby boom generation. If that brief period of our history were compared to the previous 200 years, it would be clear that the rapid growth rate was a unique and unusual occurrence. Unfortunately, an accurate perspective, including an historical population graph, does not appear in the social studies texts.

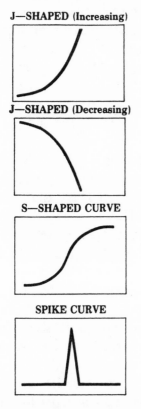

J—SHAPED (Increasing)

J—SHAPED (Decreasing)

S—SHAPED CURVE

SPIKE CURVE

J-shaped curves show a trend that starts slowly and then increases rapidly with no indication of reversal. When it increases at a constant *rate,* it is called an exponential curve.

Reversed J-shaped curves start slowly and then decrease rapidly. When it decreases at a constant *rate,* it is called an exponential curve.

S-shaped curves indicate a trend that started slowly, went through a phase of rapid change, and started to slow at some point.

Spike curves indicate a trend that maintains a low level, then takes a rapid increase and a rapid decrease, and then remains at about the same level as before the increase.

In Silver Burdett's *World Geography* (1980), a graph forecasts a world population of 6 billion in 2000 but a food supply sufficient only for a population of 4.5 billion (the 1983 world population). The projected post-1980 stagnation of food supply is not explained. This illustrates another common textbook inaccuracy in that the author generally underestimates future food supplies and overestimates consumption patterns. The typical method used in this determination is to estimate calorie consumption for a large male in a cool climate, for which there is no universal validity, and then use this sample as the basis for a projection of worldwide food consumption. But a small person working four hours a day near the equator will not consume as much as a large person working eight hours a day in cooler climes. If estimates must be made, it is far more realistic to consider the various actual calorie consumption patterns in cold, temperate, and tropical climates rather than assume some average that is a high estimate for one locale and low for another.

Some texts suggest that there is a triage system at work to determine who will eat and who will starve and that the determination is largely a function of *what* we eat. This scenario has a special appeal to guilt-ridden Westerners who believe their overeating adversely affects an undernourished peasant on the other side of the globe. In a widely circulated global studies curriculum guide, *Indiana in the World,* the teacher is instructed to give a cracker to each student and to ask who would prefer beef. If a child prefers beef, five crackers are taken away from the other students and given to him or her to illustrate the thesis that beef eaters take food away from grain eaters. Yet this conclusion is obviously not true.

This Is Our World (1981) is another text published by Silver Burdett. In it the author contends that if a planet has 10 billion acres of cropland, with the capacity to add only 3 billion more, there will be significant food supply problems. Confusing cropland with total land, the author notes that within a century 12 billion people

. . . will be trying to crowd themselves into about 13 billion acres. Of that amount, 12 billion acres will almost certainly be needed for crop raising. . . . We assume that at least five-sixths [the rest] will be needed for factories, transportation facilities, office, shopping centers, and so on. . . . That will mean that the average lot available to each of your grandchildren for building a house will be just about the size of a two-car garage.

This concern for available land, particularly farmland, ignores much of recent history. Arable land has been increasing worldwide over the past 30 years. From 1950 to 1970, a 20-year period for which there are good data, there has been a 16 percent increase in agricultural land. In the United States the conversion of farmland to housing tracts and shopping centers has been proceeding inexorably. But each year more new land is being brought into cultivation through irrigation and swamp drainage than is lost through urbanization.

Concern about the loss of farmland has led to federal restraints on new housing starts. However, these policies aren't compatible with the other government actions to keep many farms intentionally idle. In 1983, 39 percent of American crop acreage was inactive due to federal subsidy programs, at a cost of $18.3 billion to the taxpayer. It seems as if the fear of losing cropland ignores the "overproductivity" of American farmers. In the aggregate those fears about land and topsoil erosion are not put in any historical perspective. Our yields suggest that soil quality on American farms has actually been improving since the 1930s according to U.S. Department of Agriculture statistics, and if trend lines for the future are suggestive, this will remain the case for some time.

In Allyn & Bacon's *Our World and Its Peoples* (1981), however, is the claim "that perhaps half the world's people suffer from hunger most of the time." To arrive at that conclusion, the authors would have to include every weight-conscious dieter who is starving to obtain a svelte figure. Headings such as "Threats to Humanity," "Famine Throws a Shadow over the Earth," and "Blueprint for Disaster" make a mockery of the section's overall title, "Toward a Better World." Before the "Blueprint" section there is a map of world hunger with the accompanying jeremiad:

> You may have read about "four giant horsemen" galloping across the face of the earth. One stands for Famine, the second for Disease, the third for War, and the fourth for Death. Today these "four giant horsemen" are galloping more swiftly than ever before. Some people say it may already be too late to slow them down. But many, many others still do not see the danger.

Cornell University's Professor Thomas Poleman, an expert on food, recently argued that because of a variety of imponderables (such as the availability of food, nutritional requirements, and access to food based on income), predictions of famine as well as statistical projections of hunger and malnutrition are "meaningless." Nick Eberstadt of Harvard University suggests that the reported incidence of hunger is a "hype" promoted by well-meaning functionaries who work at world poverty organizations and by media people eager to dramatize the issue. One indication that this might be the case is the report of the Pan American Health Organization that concluded that more than 49 percent of the populations of Barbados, Costa Rica, Guyana, Jamaica, and Panama suffer from malnutrition. The problem with this assertion is that malnutrition, as opposed to famine, is almost impossible to measure. The one indisputable characteristic of the relative health of the population is life expectancy, a figure that has been going up steadily in these nations and is now about 70 years. This statistic casts more than a little doubt on the existence of pervasive hunger.

It is undoubtedly true that hunger is a serious problem in some parts of the world. If one were to concentrate on East Africa since political independence has been achieved, it is the one place on Earth where population growth is surging and where crops are faltering. A case can be made there for a Malthusian scenario, including starvation. In Kenya, for example, population growth is 4 percent (1983), while that of food production is 1 percent. However, this specific example doesn't alter the general picture. What is most significant in almost all the textbook cases cited is that the complexity of the hunger/population/food issue, including its many aspects and points of view and the fluctuating political conditions, is rarely presented. Globe's *Exploring World History* (1983), for example, asks the following (guilt-provoking) rhetorical questions:

Is there a limit to the number of people who can live on our planet? Scientists have discovered that when they put two mice in a cage, they get along well. When twenty mice are put in the same cage, they begin to fight each other. . . . Is the population of our earth reaching the same limit? . . . If the same rate of growth continues, the population of the earth will double in the next thirty-five years. Do you believe that all people have a right to enough food, clothing and shelter to live comfortably? Is this one of your values? Would you eat less and spend less if it meant more food for a starving person thousands of miles away? If you had a lawn or garden would you give up fertilizer so that farmers in Pakistan might grow more food?

Holt, Rinehart & Winston's *People and Our Country* (1982) states that ". . . hunger may be the biggest source of world friction in the coming decades." And Addison-Wesley's *Our Economy: How It Works* (1980) ends on this note: "Can we produce enough food to catch up with the needs of a growing population? Can we increase food production and still protect our environment?"

The implication in all of these Malthusian forecasts is that the world cannot survive in its present form due to a scenario in which the population overwhelms food and resources. To suggest that the metaphor for the globe is mice in a cage is to confuse one small aspect of nature with a comprehensive global perspective. We are not mice; anyone who thinks we are will inevitably underestimate our ability to modify the conditions of existence through human will and intelligence. Through human intelligence and ingenuity we have learned to build *up* rather than *out* to conserve space, to build a system of dams to prevent flooding, and on and on.

To assume that our space will be restricted as the population grows is also misleading. The living space in the homes of the world's people has progressively increased over the past 40 years; in the United States, for example, in 1940, 20.2 percent of the households had 1.01 or more persons per room, but in 1982 less than 4 percent reached that level.

Yet it is precisely in describing the roles of human will, intervention, and deliberate choice that the textbooks are so deficient. Nor do they offer any historical perspective from which to view short-term trends. The fact, of course, is that starvation *may* become rampant and the Earth *may* become overpopulated, but none of these is as inevitable as the social studies textbook authors would have us believe.

66

3

Energy

Spaceship Earth may be in trouble.
Follett's *Our World Today* (1983)

I t is axiomatic that we need energy to live. Food production, fertilization, irrigation, storage, transportation, and thousands of other processes require increasingly greater supplies of energy. The higher the level of industrial development (development being the aim of political and social strivings all over the globe), the higher the energy consumption per citizen. Since economic development throughout the century has been "fueled" by the consumption of energy, it has been assumed that if fossil fuels were exhausted, economic development would cease. A variation on this theme is that if the price of energy increases dramatically, the cost of production as well as prices and inflation will go up dramatically too.

This assumption—that at some point either price or supply or both will have an adverse effect on economic productivity—is based on the lessons of the period from 1973 through 1979, a time when oil prices increased tenfold, promoting a worldwide recession and, in several instances, runaway inflation. It is, therefore, not coincidental that these "lessons" were well learned by textbook authors who now write energy chapters designed to encourage an almost ascetic life-style, complete with dire admonitions that energy shortages are merely the beginning of a permanent condition of scarcity.

The one consistent theme in the texts is that energy prices are high and will continue to increase. Indeed, if one assumes that an increasingly populous world will continue to draw down dwindling energy supplies, no other conclusion is justified. The statistics used to make this case seem to support the view that our careless and selfish ways will soon exhaust the world's fossil fuels and that prices will reflect this decreasing supply and increasing demand.

However, the problem with relying on this analysis is that estimates of energy supply are complicated. In the textbooks there seems to be confusion written into discussions of "estimated recoverable supplies" of energy reserves. Follett's *World Geography* (1983) notes that "some experts say our known reserves will last only twenty-five or thirty years. Even if new wells are found, oil supplies may not last much longer than fifty years at the very most." But "known reserves" are not defined. In an Addison-Wesley text, *Our Economy: How It Works* (1980), we read that "we use up a little more of the world's petroleum resources every day." Laidlaw's *Free Enterprise—The American Economic System* (1981) also emphasizes scarcity and in at least three places refers to "exhaustion of resources" without providing any explanation or documentation for that assertion.

Without putting statements like these into the proper context, they sound unduly ominous. There is little question that at some point we will run out of oil. There is probably no denying that. But there is probably more oil available to us than the textbook authors would have us believe. There is the distinct probability that energy-efficient equipment will stretch the existing supply. There are alternatives that have been developed and that will be developed that can compensate for a shortage of oil. We don't know when this depletion will occur. And it should also be noted that new reserves are still being found and that conservation has had a significant impact on the level of energy use. But this is rarely what one reads.

Follett's *Our World Today* (1983) treats energy in a section titled "The Worldwide Cry for Natural Resources" and again resorts to the common (and misleading) concept of "Spaceship Earth":

Spaceship Earth may be in trouble. The number of passengers on board has increased. These passengers have consumed more and more of our ship's natural resources. The supply crew has informed us that some of our resources are running low. We must learn to use our remaining supplies wisely. We must learn to practice conservation. . . . What can one person do . . .? Individuals can stop wasting the resources they use. We can help by recycling our mineral resources. . . . Individuals can use less energy in their homes and for transportation.

While the authors of this text rightly advise caution in using resources, they confuse the static supply of energy on a spaceship with the almost infinite supply of ideas on Earth that can be used to generate resource substitutes. It is the ability to discover substitutes and extend the life of reserves through human ingenuity that is excluded from most textbook accounts.

This theme of "disappearing fuel" is further explored in Silver Burdett's *This Is Our World* (1981). At the beginning of the volume the author reveals his bias with the subtitle "Our Vanishing Resources." It includes the following reference to "disappearing riches":

Our metal-using, fuel-burning civilization is built upon a vanishing asset, the riches that have accumulated over hundreds of millions of years in the earth's crust. . . . We do not stop to think how new cars and thermostats are. Two or three generations ago, they did not exist. A few generations from now they may have disappeared. . . . Every day our natural resources are becoming scarce. . . . We ought not to say to ourselves how lucky we are to live in this age of machines, power, abundant food, and comfortable homes. Rather, we should ask how long our luck will last.

This statement is extraordinary; it is based on the assumption that our wealth and advantages are functions of luck. Luck, as we know, is capricious and transitory. To emphasize a throw of the dice is to subordinate personal effort and enterprise to sheer happenstance. Why should young people admire our system, or be willing to defend it, when it is not a creation of labor, effort, enterprise, and imagination? Why should anyone work hard to promote his or her own future if success is based on luck? It is curious that the same texts that make these arguments cite ingenuity and imagination as part of entrepreneurship. The person who can invent technology for the extension of oil supplies or who can find an inexpensive way to use waves to manufacture electricity will be a wealthy person indeed. One wonders, however, why these textbook authors adopt a static view of resources if ingenuity is one of its characteristics? The implication of the textbook arguments such as those cited above is that fossil fuels will soon disappear. Invariably authors who accept this gloomy prognosis question why we can't curb our appetites (the implicit assumption being that we can't) and what will happen when essential resources run out (the implicit assumption being that they will). Yet very few writers recognize the quite reasonable possibility that there are products in the ground and in space whose value to us is unknown at the moment but that may well alleviate the "depletion" of oil. Did anyone in the nineteenth century know there was uranium in the ground, that it had value, and that it was a source of energy?

In the wonderful children's story of Chicken Little, Chicken runs around warning everybody that "the sky is falling in." In some form or other, prodded by a million different issues, doomsayers have always predicted catastrophes. Nineteenth-century "Chicken Littles" argued that the disappearance of whale oil would mark the end of American civilization; in 1973, with the establishment of the OPEC cartel, cries about the fall of the industrialized nations due to oil shortages could be heard around the world. Once again the doomsayers were wrong, but their predictions and conclusions live in our textbooks and therefore in the minds of the young.

An economic system such as ours is driven by hard work, ingenuity, and the profit motive. If the price of oil increases because of supply interruptions, marginal oil fields become potentially profitable, other fossil fuels become reasonable alternatives, an incentive to develop synthetic fuels emerges, and unorthodox sources of energy (for example, solar and thermal) become competitive. "Vanishing energy resources" is a meaningless phrase unless one considers the way in which their "disappearance" promotes the exploration for alternatives. Yet even in economic texts this isn't explained.

If one considers a "resource" part labor, part technology, and part capital, then the application of capital to labor-saving technology should enhance the productivity of energy sources in the future. In other words, technological advances will improve the feasibility of using the sun, or the heat in the ground, or the waves at sea as energy sources. They will also improve the feasibility and safety of using breeder reactors. For example, extracting oil from shale was not possible until new technologies were introduced. Similarly, using peat to produce fuel—a process known for decades—didn't become cost-effective until the price of oil became higher than the cost of peat distillation.

Although this description of energy in the future is decidedly more positive than most textbook presentations, it is not intended to minimize either the problems we had in the 1970s or the sometimes painful readjustments of the 1980s. However, it should be recognized—and rarely is—that while an "oil shock" such as that in 1973 can create economic difficulties, *it also can relieve them.* As prices steadily increase, marginal wells once too expensive to exploit become productive. The incentive to find energy alternatives is compelling. (The oil embargo of 1973 promoted the use of coal as an energy alternative, a fossil fuel whose known reserve can last at least several hundred years.) And economic pressure to conserve is enhanced. Most important, the idea that a difficulty also can be an opportunity is seldom considered in textbooks that encourage a decidedly pessimistic outlook. Textbooks uniformly ignore the distinguishing characteristics between short-term energy projections that often require difficult adjustments and long-term projections that allow for policy alternatives. From 1973 to 1981 the industrialized states suffered from an economic recession due in no small part to the high price of energy. Over the long term (the next 20 years) one can construct a credible energy scenario in which alternatives gradually replace oil and the difficult adjustments of the 1970s become incorporated into general business practices relieving the pressure on energy expenses.

Laidlaw's *The Challenge of Freedom* (1982), a U.S. history text, includes an excerpt from an M.I.T. scholar who argues:

My conclusion . . . is that world oil will run short sooner than people realize. Unless appropriate remedies are applied soon, the demand for petroleum in the non-Communist world will probably overtake supplies around 1985 to 1995. That is the maximum time we have. . . . It might be less. Petroleum demand could exceed supply as early as 1983 if the OPEC countries maintain the present production ceilings.

There are several questions worth asking about this assertion: Primarily, why did a book published in 1982 make no mention of an oil glut that was already forcing world markets prices down and the market adjustments that constitute "appropriate remedies"? Is the term "non-Communist" used to suggest that Communist nations are more careful about energy use than we are? And what leads the author to the conclusion that demand probably will overtake supply between 1985 and 1995, when conservation measures have already been effective and alternative sources are increasingly being utilized?

Macmillan's *History of a Free People* (1981) is equally dogmatic in its assertions regarding "the oil crisis":

> The oil crisis was met by various stopgap measures. . . . But there was *no rationing,* and Americans *were not compelled to give up their wasteful habits.* The oil crisis made the public suddenly aware that world supplies of petroleum were running out. Unless a new source of cheap energy could be found, the automobile era was approaching its end. It was a time for serious *long-range planning,* but little was done [my emphases].

It is surprising that rationing would still be considered a reasonable option after government efforts to supervise the oil supply in 1979. There is little evidence that gas station oil quotas imposed by Washington bureaucrats alleviated the temporary supply shortage. Barring a serious national emergency, the data suggest that pricing rather than economic engineering can produce the desired consumer response. Rarely, however, does one find this issue discussed in economic terms in social studies textbooks. This same Macmillan text concludes the section on energy with this ominous prediction: "Having become accustomed to abundance and affluence the United States now seemed to face an age of diminishing resources and economic uncertainties."

Laidlaw's *A History of Our American Public* (1981) includes a similar prognosis:

In the years ahead many Americans may have to do without goods or activities that use scarce energy materials. This may be needed to make sure that other generations will not be left without valuable natural resources.

At no point in either of these books is the issue of market adjustments discussed.

A discussion question at the end of the energy section in the Laidlaw book asks pointedly: "Why will it be necessary to alter United States society as the future approaches?" The answer, learned from the text, is because we have been wasteful, careless, and greedy. Children reading this obviously can't feel very good about their future or their past. But the history of the past 200 years demonstrates something very different from this textbook treatment. When energy sources (for example, whale oil) in the past were depleted, a search for alternatives commenced. In the short run the impact was harsh, but over the long term, adjustments were made in the form of substitutes and conservation. This historical picture does not ensure the duplication of events in the future, but it does provide a context from which to consider present and future problems. That, however, also is rarely found in textbook treatments of the issue.

In Rand McNally's *The Promise of Democracy: The Grand Experiment* (1978), we read the following:

Americans would have to change their whole style of life before they could save the land and its resources. Few people seemed willing to give up the things that make life a little easier. Despite warnings of power shortages, Americans continued to buy electric air conditioners, can openers, pencil sharpeners, and even toothbrushes.

The authors, as is the case in other examples cited here, give no indication of the remarkable resilience of Americans—that is, our ability to cope with energy disruptions in the past and the development of new technology to help close the supply gap when it exists. Shortages in the past have not lead to a permanent change in the national character, merely to a temporary change of relatively small significance. Here again, however, historical perspective (in the form of trend lines) is omitted.

What can be found instead is an effort to seize the "shortage" argument to propagandize for government regulation. There is the recurring belief that we must be frightened or shamed into recognizing the dimensions of the problem; curbing our appetite is deemed to be a hopeless exercise unless the power of government coercion is unleashed. Missing from these scenarios is any recognition of the way in which Americans have responded to energy supply problems in the distant past or disruptions in the recent past.

Also missing is the need to question the existence of "shortages." For example, it is difficult to find a text that notes we have only scraped the surface of known coal deposits. Worldwide coal reserves are estimated at 10 trillion tons; approximately 690 billion of these can presently be extracted at a reasonable cost, with the likelihood that technological advances in the future will lower the expense substantially for the rest of these reserves. Even with an increase in consumption, coal supplies will last for many hundreds of years. In addition, a likely improvement in liquefaction and gasification techniques will extend this future even further, a projection widely accepted by experts in the fossil fuel business. The known deposits of uranium and thorium, additional sources of energy, are far greater than coal, oil, and natural-gas resources combined.

Any projection of energy supply in the future would have to consider a rapid expansion in the use of coal, nuclear power, synthetic fuels, heavy oils and tars, and a phasing out of oil and gas in the production of electricity. Solar energy is likely to remain an unimportant immediate source of energy because the price of other fuels will remain low into the next century.

The demand for energy will increase, with estimates indicating that the annual use of coal will go up 3.8 times and that nuclear power use will increase by a factor of 76 by the end of the century. But the picture is not one of unceasing growth in demand. Economic growth rates in the United States and other major industrialized nations are likely to decline, while those rates in developing states attempting to modernize will increase. In other words, the textbook assumption of a constant rate of growth for developed and developing nations alike is seriously flawed, a fact that has a direct bearing on estimates of likely energy use in the future.

Even in the case where oil and gas prices do not rise, these energy resources will be available for at least another 50 years, and the petroleum supply is likely to keep up with the demand until some time in the next century. At that point the price will be very expensive unless alternative sources become available at competitive prices. The point here is that energy shortages and rising prices are not the central problems to be faced by this generation of students; they are transitional issues that require adjustments in the market and in the human capacity for innovation. The problem for students is to contemplate some of the options and alternatives that can help make the transition relatively problem-free.

People as different in viewpoint as Barry Commoner, an avowed environmentalist, and Julian Simon, a critic of many Club of Rome and *Global 2000 Report* predictions, agree that energy shortages are greatly exaggerated. Commoner stated in *The Poverty of Power* (1976):

> Certainly with respect to energy there is no evidence that our present problems stem from a shortage in that resource. There is enough petroleum in the United States to meet all our needs for at least the next fifty years.

Simon noted in *The Ultimate Resource* (1981):

> There is no compelling theoretical reason why we should eventually run out of energy, or even why energy should be more scarce and costly in the future than it is now.

Yet this opinion by experts with widely divergent views does not make the grade with textbook writers.

Nuclear energy usually is considered an evil in textbooks, an energy alternative for people concerned only with satisfying their immediate appetites and unconcerned with the general health and safety of future generations. However, nuclear energy currently accounts for between 2 and 3 percent of the world's total energy production with no significant damage to its beneficiaries (including those around Three Mile Island). Despite the exaggerated claim of meltdown at Three Mile Island, government reports afterward indicated that the level of radiation vented during the height of the "crisis" was lower than the routine daily expiration of radiation from Dutch and French nuclear energy reactors. The hazard to the health of Harrisburg residents was roughly equivalent to the radiation experienced during a chest X ray. And this was during a man-made crisis in which almost every conceivable human blunder was made. If one wants to compare the relative safety of nuclear plants with electrical energy production and coal mining, it is useful to examine comparative deaths in these industries. Each year coal mining kills thousands, electrical energy hundreds, and nuclear energy a handful.

This comparison, of course, does not take into account potential destruction in nuclear plants, because that is speculation. People *might* die from a nuclear energy plant accident, but they *are* dying as a result of coal mining (and without any significant outcry from the public). Moreover, in the next 15 or 20 years fusion reactors will be available that are potentially highly reliable and have negligible radiation risk.

My argument is not a plea for nuclear energy plants. I merely suggest that this option is rarely considered as a positive energy alternative in textbooks. It would seem reasonable that if fossil fuels were being exhausted and energy were needed for our survival, every energy alternative would be given serious consideration. One would hope that voters could weigh risks and benefits with some idea of why they elected to say "No" or "Yes." Our students, however, usually are given one side of this controversy, with nuclear energy protrayed as the devil's brew.

If one were to consider all the present and possible sources of energy including oil, coal, shale, tar sands, methanol, liquefaction, gasification, nuclear, solar, thermal, fusion, natural gas, hydroelectric, and peat, and then consider conservation methods, petroleum technology, and human ingenuity, a compelling case can be made for a future with a great many beneficent energy possibilities and greatly reduced energy costs. Even from a purely geological perspective, most of the world has not yet been seriously explored for oil. The potential for finding new sources may be surprisingly great. Several geologists have suggested that exploration should be intensified outside of North

America, the Middle East, Western Europe, and the USSR; discoveries in the new areas are possible, and the resultant payoffs may be very significant.

This hopeful but realistic vision is based on the conjunction of several factors, including political and economic incentives to find new energy sources and to develop new energy technology. As is always the case, there are risks. If oil costs spiral downward very quickly, there will be far less motivation to search for or experiment with new energy sources. It may be very myopic to abandon exploration and synthetic development even if the price doesn't warrant such action at the moment. Then there are risks imposed by international disorder. Can we protect our vital oil interests if threatened by a potent Soviet blue-water navy, or by a hostile regime in an oil-rich nation? And do we calculate into the price of a barrel of oil the cost of protecting the sea lanes between oil-rich nations and our allies?

The problem as I see it is that the economic and political difficulties of the "energy problem" are left out of the textbooks as routinely as the negative outlook is put in. Neither realistic prospects nor plausible risks are presented in contemporary texts. Energy shortages have become a useful symbol for textbook authors who choose to describe a nation that squanders its natural bounty without any regard for the consequences to the environment or to future generations. Unfortunately, the symbol often is a substitute for careful analysis. In the case of energy only one side of a complex matter is discussed, and that is surely insufficient either to understand or to discuss the issue intelligently.

4

Minerals

The labour of nature is paid not because she does much, but because he does little. In proportion as she becomes niggardly in her gifts, he exacts a greater price for her gifts.

David Ricardo, *Principles of Political Economy and Taxation* (1817)

I t is usually assumed that minerals cannot last forever. In addition, as they are depleted through continued exploitation, a point will be reached when their price will be prohibitively high. This is Ricardo's equation presented as an immutable law of nature. The contemporary vision of a similar argument equating disappearing resources with increasing prices received its most compelling testimony in the *Limits to Growth* report (1972). Its authors claim that even with the most optimistic assumptions about technology and replacement, our basic raw materials will be prohibitively expensive in 100 years, our way of life will be jeopardized by the disappearance of these raw materials, and the epoch of unchecked material growth will draw to a close due to resource depletion. This scenario is very much like the one presented in recent high school social studies texts.

However, the notion of "finite" natural resources is misleading. Natural resources, or raw materials, are not given once and for all; as some are used, others come into being. Both terms refer only to materials that are accessible and can currently be exploited; they represent only a fraction of total supply. The total supply, or "deposits," represent resources that cannot yet be exploited either because the price of extraction would be excessive, the appropriate technology doesn't exist, or the location of the deposit makes transportation costs prohibitive and mining procedures formidable. As price and technology factors change, so do our estimates of natural resources. A resource is inextricably related to what can be exploited at a certain time.

Most textbooks neither explain this point nor explain that in "real" terms (controlling for inflation) most minerals have become increasingly less expensive as the demand for them has increased. Yet many of the claims about minerals present the Ricardo/*Limits to Growth* scenario of rapidly and inexorably rising prices, with increasing demand and decreasing supply.

Even the recent report prepared during the Carter administration, *Global 2000,* projects a 5 percent yearly increase in the real price of nonfuel minerals until the year 2000. Most textbooks still rely on David Ricardo's concept of diminishing returns in which extraction of minerals from less productive land becomes increasingly more costly. It is precisely this "law" that underlies the assumption of arrested economic growth. At some point—if this scenario is believed—raw materials will become scarce and industrial development will be curtailed. The same assumption inspired Karl Marx to consider the inevitability of social conflict between the owners of the means of production and the laborers. Marx's labor theory of value emerges, in part, from the perception that the bourgeoisie must extract more from the workers to account for the increasingly marginal utility of the land.

However, this theory, which seems logical and plausible, is consistently contradicted by human experience. Between 1950 and 1970 alone, there has been a 4,000 percent increase in known mineral reserves.

	How "Known Reserves" Alter		
Ore	Known Reserves in 1950 (1,000 Metric Tons)	Known Reserves in 1970 (1,000 Metric Tons)	Percent Increase
Iron	19,000,000	251,000,000	1,321
Manganese	500,000	635,000	27
Chromite	100,000	775,000	675
Tungsten	1,903	1,328	− 30
Copper	100,000	279,000	179
Lead	40,000	86,000	115
Zinc	70,000	113,000	61
Tin	6,000	6,600	10
Bauxite	1,400,000	5,300,000	279

How "Known Reserves" Alter *(cont'd.)*

Ore	Known Reserves in 1950 (1,000 Metric Tons)	Known Reserves in 1970 (1,000 Metric Tons)	Percent Increase
Potash	5,000,000	118,000,000	2,360
Phosphates	26,000,000	1,178,000,000	4,430
Oil	75,000,000	455,000,000	507

Source: Council on International Economic Policy, Executive Office of the President, 1974.

By any relevant measure the trend is toward less scarcity and lower prices rather than the reverse. In fact, the costs of almost every natural resource have trended downward over the course of recorded history.

These trends suggest that raw materials are becoming increasingly available, especially when compared with the most fundamental characteristic of economic life, human work-time. The prices of raw materials have been falling in comparison to those of consumer goods and to the Consumer Price Index. To demonstrate how significant this price reduction has been, the decrease in the cost of raw materials is greater than the decrease in the cost of those consumer items produced with the increasingly efficient use of labor and capital. But even if the prices of raw materials were rising in comparison with those of consumer goods, the raw materials still would be taking a progressively smaller proportion of our income.

Moreover, even this positive fact concerning the accessibility of raw materials understates the case. We have learned to employ less of the raw materials. The copper pot we once used for cooking probably is made of a less-expensive aluminum alloy. A single communications satellite in space provides intercontinental telephone connections that would otherwise require thousands of tons of copper.

There are, of course, reasons why the relative price of nonfuels may rise over time. These include the nationalization of mineral companies; environmental controls (particularly stringent land-use policies); natural disasters; and decreased access to water for mineral processing. But even if all of these were to occur, the price increases necessary to accommodate them are unlikely to be very great since these conditions have been anticipated or have happened before an adjustment can occur without the prodding of great price increases. In addition, the minerals most threatened by these occurrences—cobalt, copper, nickel, and manganese—can be derived from deep-sea nodules once undersea mining technology is cost-effective or once the increasing price of the minerals makes it cost-effective.

Clearly no economy can absorb with absolute equanimity a sudden disruption in supply, where disruptions occur so unexpectedly there is no time to adjust. But when one considers the number of potential suppliers, the substitutes that are being discovered, and new technologies, it is hard to construct a credible short-term scarcity scenario of almost any natural resource.

Nonetheless, Follett's *World Geography* (1983) includes this statement:

> In today's industrial societies, the use of minerals is increasing rapidly. The resources of minerals in the world were once thought to be almost endless. Now people are not so sure of their continued abundance.

Silver Burdett's *This Is Our World* (1981) makes the erroneous claim that "the cost of mining is always increasing." Allyn & Bacon's *Magruder's American Government* (1982) asks students to consider the consequences of the nation's reluctance to follow

Teddy Roosevelt's advice on the stewardship of natural resources. The teacher guide has the apparent answer: "Most students will likely define the price [of ignoring T.R.'s injunction] in
terms of the present and future consequences of the irretrievable
loss of much of the nation's forest resources, agricultural lands
and mineral supplies from short-sighted exploitation and wasteful use."

Harcourt Brace Jovanovich's *American Civics* (1979) argues:

Americans have covered the land with cement and asphalt,
buildings and highways. As the number of people grew, houses
spread into the countryside where, often, precious farmland
gave way to new buildings. To meet our demand for goods,
mountains have been stripped bare for lumber and for coal,
copper, silver, gold, and other minerals.

This statement might almost be headlined "America's Rape of
Mother Earth." The beneficial consequences of highways, buildings, and consumer goods are omitted entirely, as is a depiction of
what our nation would be like without the so-called exploitation
of the Earth's minerals.

That we should be prudent in our use of mineral resources is
not unreasonable. It is the point of the following excerpt from
Macmillan's *Global Geography* (1981):

Many people who have studied resource scarcity believe that
simply applying more technology to the problem is not
enough. . . . According to this theory, we must learn to accept
limits to growth. Instead of living by such mottoes as "bigger is
better," we might consider, as some suggest, that "less is more"
and that "small is beautiful."

In this same vein but at a slightly higher evangelical pitch, Prentice-Hall's *The United States: Combined Edition* (1982) makes this claim:

Raised on the gospel of progress, few wanted to be told that there were limits to the nation's capacities, powers, and natural resources; that they must lower their expectations and aspirations; that they would need to exercise self-discipline and be prepared to make sacrifices.

On the face of it there is little in this argument to contest, despite its preaching tone. Conservation may indeed be necessary. But preaching is all too often a substitute for accurate analysis of economic issues or a serious review of future mineral availability. If the following table, extracted from a Resource for The Future pamphlet, is accurate, world consumption rates for nonfuel minerals are likely to decline in the next 40 years, albeit the rate of decline is uneven.

World Consumption and Rates of Growth in Consumption of Nonfuel Minerals, 1971, and Projected Growth Rates, Standard Case

	Absolute Figures in Thousands of Tons	Annual Percentage Rates of Growth		
	1971	1971–85	1985–2000	2000–25
Aluminum	12,107	6.7	4.8	4.4
Chromium	3,416	2.5	2.5	2.6
Cobalt	44	4.4	2.9	3.2
Copper	8,026	2.9	2.1	2.1
Iron in ore	456,183	2.3	2.2	2.3
Lead	4,768	3.1	2.7	2.5
Manganese	2,786	6.0	3.6	3.7
Molybdenum	40	7.4	3.4	3.3

World Consumption and Rates of Growth in Consumption of Nonfuel Minerals, 1971, and Projected Growth Rates, Standard Case *(cont'd.)*

	Absolute Figures in Thousands of Tons	Annual Percentage Rates of Growth		
	1971	1971–85	1985–2000	2000–25
Nickel	657	4.7	3.6	3.5
Phosphate rock	114,913	3.2	2.6	2.0
Potash	21,711	2.8	2.2	1.9
Sulfur	24,251	4.5	3.6	2.9
Tin	257	3.1	2.6	2.8
Titanium	543	9.2	4.5	3.7
Tungsten	23	4.9	2.9	3.1
Vanadium	22	4.7	3.4	3.0
Zinc	5,525	3.3	2.6	2.7

Source: Ronald Ridker, *Resource and Environmental Consequences of Population and Economic Growth,* Resource for The Future (1972), p. 102.

In a 1977 United Nations study conducted by a team of researchers led by Nobel Prize winner, Wassily Leontief, the following was argued:

Known world resources of metallic minerals . . . are generally sufficient to supply world requirements through the remaining decades of this century, and probably into the early part of the next century as well. . . . Mineral resource endowment is generally adequate to support world economic development at relatively high rates.

And an OECD report *Interfuture: Facing the Future* (1979), concluded:

Overall physical scarcity of industrial raw materials through natural depletion of resources *is not a likely eventuality.* . . . As long as the economic and technical course of events is not disturbed by sudden unforeseeable breaks, the concern often expressed on this score need not be subscribed to [emphasis in the original].

Yet almost without exception, textbook authors have ignored these reports and instead have adopted the position that raw materials soon will be exhausted. They do not even attempt to substantiate their claim but simply adopt the 1972 Club of Rome position and present it as the new gospel. Even if they were correct (if exaggerated) arguments that could be made at the time, most of the alarmist prognoses are by now superseded by events, and some of the statements have been retracted by the authors themselves. But not by the textbook writers. Why is there such a time lag between "current events" texts and current events?

One of the essential reasons for misjudging mineral supplies has to do with models used by researchers—models generally developed for only one purpose. For example, a model intended to estimate the price and use of cobalt in a year probably will provide worse results than no model at all for predicting cobalt prices and use in five or 10 years. This is because market forces and alternatives take years to evolve and generally are not factored into short-term models.

Nobel Prize winner Gunnar Myrdal contended that modeling of the kind used in the Club of Rome report is unrelated to scientific veracity:

[T]he use of mathematical equations and a huge computer, which registers the alternatives of abstractly conceived policies by a "world simulation model," may impress the innocent general public but has little, if any, scientific validity. That this "sort of model is actually a new tool for mankind" is unfortunately not true. It represents quasi-learnedness of a type that we have, for a long time, had too much of, not least in economics, when we try to deal with problems simply in economic terms.

Another point that modelers usually ignore is that there is no incentive either to look for or to develop new sources of raw materials when known reserves are plentiful. Under normal circumstances there is no reason to expect the rate of exploration (for new sources) to exceed the rate of consumption (of current sources). It is possible to construct a model of eventual mineral exhaustion if one projects figures far enough into the future, but that kind of extrapolation doesn't allow for total reserves, nor does it consider the impact of price on supply and consumption. One can talk about "running out" of a mineral, but the real meaning of that claim is that the *price* of extracting the mineral (which may be abundant) is prohibitively high. For example, one could argue by using known reserves and present consumption patterns that aluminum will be in very short supply by about 2050. However, what is not noted in this calculation is that: only bauxite sources have been included in "known reserves"; a decrease in demand can stretch existing supplies; and 8.3 percent of the Earth's crust is composed of aluminum in other forms, making it one of the most abundant structural metals on the globe. Somewhere between a 20 and an 80 percent increase in the price of bauxite would be required to justify switching to nonbauxite sources using today's technology. That would require a significant market adjustment but would not signal an economic catastrophe. Moreover, a potential price increase of that magnitude would serve as a catalyst for the rapid pursuit of aluminum replacements.

Let us look at a hypothetical case of "running out" of a

mineral. Assume copper reserves were being depleted but still could be extracted from rarefied sources at a very high price. Assume further that the price remained high and the need for copper remained great. At this point an incentive to develop the appropriate extraction technology would be equally great. Now assume, for the sake of argument, that copper resources in the ground have been exhausted. If that were to happen, copper "above ground"—wires, pipes, coins, etc.—would be sold at a premium. The value of the available copper would elicit a market response to sell, and to substitute zinc, tin, and other less-expensive metals for copper.

But now assume an even more implausible situation—that one no longer could find copper either below or above ground. Here is where the theory of "market adaptability" becomes particularly salient. If copper cannot be used in communication systems, then a substitute—for example, a satellite—can be sought. If copper cannot be used in pennies, then either substitute metals can be found or plastic cards can be designed that could be used as specie (or we could go back to beads and wampum). If television images cannot be conducted along a coaxial cable with copper wiring, then fiber optics may be used instead. If copper can't be used in pipes, then an alloy of aluminum and steel can be substituted.

The copper example illustrates that the combination of technology, capital, and enterprise can offset models of "inevitable scarcity." Coincidentally, the illustration suggests an explanation for the present depressed price of copper, a mineral that in the late 1950s was considered a relatively scarce resource.

To some extent, the depletion of a resource is immediately seen in its price—assuming demand remains constant—and market forces are set in motion to redress the supply problem. This system is not perfect, but if the evidence of the past 200 years is a guide, it works.

The adaptation of the market when faced with supply shortages and the distinction between "deposits" and "known reserves" are vital factors in any discussion of resources. Yet neither is systematically considered in social studies textbooks. Instead, minerals are characterized as "finite," mankind's greed is "insatiable," and the combination leads (explicitly or implicitly) to economic "disaster." The historical record on these matters is virtually ignored and, more important, almost no attention is paid to the ways in which the economic world really works.

5

Environment

We are witnessing once again the emergence of the view of the environment and development as rival players. . . . This point of view completely misses the recognition that production patterns which pay little heed to environmental degradation or resource depletion are ultimately doomed and in their dying may create enormous and irreversible ecological havoc.

Soedjatmoko, Rector, United Nations University

During the past 20 years, concern for the environment has elicited a vigorous reaction by the American public. Serious efforts to clean up pollution have resulted in a spate of state and federal laws to deal with the problem. And these efforts have brought about substantial improvements. But this does not mean that pollution no longer exists, or that some of the more intractable issues (for example, disposal of toxic wastes) have been handled well. Nor does it mean that the natural gifts of air and water won't continue to be degraded as demand for them grows.

What the experience of the recent past does suggest is that the serious dimensions of environmental problems often can be counteracted by concern and good management, and if necessary by imposing governmental taxes and fines to keep the environment relatively clean. However, what one usually reads about is ecological shock and environmental vulnerability and about the terrible consequences of abusing the fragility of ecological systems. This point of view is well expressed in *The Global 2000 Report* (1980):

> If present trends continue, the world in 2000 will be more crowded, more polluted, less stable ecologically, and more vulnerable to disruption than the world we live in now. Serious stresses involving population, resources, and environment are clearly visible ahead. . . . Barring revolutionary advances in technology, life for most people on earth will be more precarious in 2000 than it is now—unless the nations of the world act decisively to alter current trends.

Most textbooks discuss environmental problems in tones that range from intemperate to hysterical. If these adjectives appear to be exaggerated, consider the following quotes and the fact that there are no accompanying citations for these claims, nor is there an historical context for evaluating their veracity.

Silver Burdett's *This Is Our World* (1981) makes this argument:

Without the winds that keep most of this "fallout" [pollution] from actually falling into the layer of surface air we breathe, every man, woman and child in the world would be dead or dying.

In another Silver Burdett geography textbook this claim is made:

It is possible that the buildup of carbon dioxide in the atmosphere may reduce the heat of the sun. That could mean the end of everything we value in modern civilization. . . . We are playing a game against our environment. The stakes are high—no less than the survival of the human race. . . . Do we have any "plays" that nature cannot block? Can we ever win this grim game with our environment?

Follett's *Our World Today* (1983) notes:

In heavily populated areas . . . land, water and air pollution are increasing to dangerously high levels.

Macmillan's *Global Geography* (1981) maintains:

Modern societies destroy the habitat at an alarming rate. . . . Coal smoke can . . . cause global temperatures to rise. Poisonous chemicals dumped underground can seep through the soil into water supplies to threaten whole populations. . . .

Jacque Cousteau . . . believes that the oceans have become permanently polluted from oil spills and industrial wastes. If this is so, ocean currents can carry that pollution to every corner of the globe.

Merrill's *Global Insights: People and Cultures* (1980) argues:

Some rivers and lakes had become so polluted with industrial waste that fish could no longer live in them. Some foods had become dangerous to eat because of the indiscriminate use of lethal chemicals. The air had become filled with poisonous fumes from automobiles, and smoke covered some cities like a gray shroud. It often seemed a war was going on between humans and nature. Increasing numbers of people realized that—in the end—they would not be the victors.

Harcourt Brace Jovanovich's *Rise of the American Nation* (1977) characterizes the environmental problem as follows:

Clean air in many cities had been replaced by smog. Some rivers had been turned into virtual sewers. . . . Fertile farmland had been bulldozed to build highways and housing developments. Much of the once beautiful American countryside had been destroyed. . . . Moreover, pollution may involve still deadlier hazards. . . . The contamination of the oceans could eventually alter or even destroy nature's global life support system.

Rand McNally's *The Promise of Democracy* (1978) begins a section entitled "One Last Chance" with a 1920s poem by Don Marquis that includes such lines as: "It won't be long now, it won't be long/till earth is barren as the moon."

Harper & Row's *A People and a Nation* (1981) argues:

Ugliness, junk, clutter, and noise scream for attention. What
solution is there to "too much" of everything? . . . While
billions were spent on the moon shot and the war in Vietnam,
problems of public life mounted. The United States, like other
industrial countries, was plagued by pollution of the water
and the air, by a pressing need for more parks, schools,
playgrounds, hospitals, by a decline in public order and
safety, and by hideous graveyards of abandoned cars. . . .
Strong regulations protecting our national resources and
controlling pollution may be needed to avert a possible ecological disaster. Yet industry sees such measures as being too
restrictive.

Harcourt Brace Jovanovich's *American Civics* (1979) makes
this point:

Changes in the makeup of the air, some scientists say, are
changing the earth's climate. Harmful gases and tiny particles
of foreign matter are increasing the upper atmosphere. When
the sun's rays strike these particles, the rays are scattered back
into space. It will not take long, these scientists say, for this
process to cut down the amount of sunlight that reaches the
earth. The effect of this will be to reduce plant life and,
eventually, to threaten all life on earth.

Macmillan's *History of a Free People* (1981) uses Stewart
Udall's phrase "the quiet crisis" to describe a section on the
environment and underscores the magnitude of the problem by
alleging: "There is increasing awareness that human beings,

especially affluent human beings like the Americans, threaten to make the earth unlivable."

Harcourt Brace Jovanovich's *The Development of American Economic Life* (1978) asks "Will the Earth Remain Livable?" and answers, ". . . [S]ome scientists fear that the growing amount of heat generated by industrial processes may change the earth's climate with potentially catastrophic effects."

Merrill's *Economics: Principles and Practices* (1981) maintains:

> The problem of pollution is not confined to the United States. The globe is covered with a belt of filth, and as the earth travels it picks up additional millions of tons of pollutants. Some scientists estimate that the average temperature of this planet will rise by seven degrees within twenty-five years due to the blanket of air pollution which keeps heat from escaping into space. This "greenhouse effect" will result in some melting of polar ice caps. . . . [T]he sea level will rise dangerously. It would not take much of a rise to completely flood large sections of this country.

Throughout these texts is the recurring question of whether the Earth will be habitable in the future. This is not simply academic speculation for textbook authors or imaginative students; an uninhabitable Earth is seen as a real possibility. After all, if forests are denuded and farmland is fast disappearing, what other conclusions can one possibly derive? Lakes are dying, fish are dead, spray cans are destroying a shield of protective elements that surround the Earth, and gases and acid vapors are attacking stone buildings in our cities and organs in our bodies. A delicate ecological balance has been upset by man's presumed ignorance, greed, and insensitivity to nature. In these texts, industrial and governmental leaders are depicted as unenlightened individuals who think living space is unlimited and the environment is indestructible. No wonder they seemingly have no qualms about harming what they believe is either easily replaced or bountiful beyond our imagination.

These characterizations—of the degree of environmental damage and the insensitivity of our leaders—are grossly exaggerated and in most instances unsubstantiated. Certainly, to live without regard for one's environment will eventually lead to a deterioration in the quality of life. Surely there are people whose disregard for others causes damage to the environment—one example on a very small scale is people who throw refuse into the street instead of a receptacle. No one can defend these actions. But this is not the way in which most people conduct their lives.

Nonetheless, some trade-offs may have to be made. Business and political leaders of this and other countries often face hard decisions. For example, maybe pollution of a local stream from a wood-processing plant is justified by the overall improved standard of living for the plant's employees and the town's residents. One would prefer industrial development without any pollution, but that desirable goal is not always possible. As a result, economic and social trade-offs have to be considered.

Improvements in the standard of living or the environment usually come at a price. We may not want to pay it, but there are consequences for inaction. The textbooks, however, often depict gains without risks, or suggest that risks are not worth taking regardless of the consequences.

It may well be that certain risks are not worth taking. If Long Island residents resist the opening of the Shoreham nuclear power plant, they will have to consider rising costs for electricity produced through more expensive means. That may be the right decision, but it is a decision wherein the economic, environmental, and emotional costs must be considered.

To suggest that all options with various degrees of risk are ill considered is a prescription for stagnation; on environmental issues, in particular, it seems impossible (and unwise) to proceed only in those areas where the potential of damage is negligible. It is a position that can do the nation and individuals harm. One could have argued at the turn of the century that a new, miraculous means of transportation could be developed that would revolutionize our nation—however, it came with a price tag of 55,000 deaths a year. If this innovation had been rejected the lives might have been saved, but the automobile would not be in existence.

Textbook authors rarely consider this kind of trade-off. Moreover, their analysis of environmental issues includes several egregious errors. For example, carbon dioxide does *not* have a cooling effect on the climate, as was suggested in Silver Burdett's geography text cited above. Cutting down the trees and shrubs in a rain forest does *not* noticeably reduce the supply of oxygen in the atmosphere, since the debris on the forest floor consumes as much oxygen as the foliage respiration releases. Yet this misconception appears in Macmillan's *Global Geography* (1981), which doesn't even point out the ways in which oxygen is released into the atmosphere.

Similarly, exaggerated claims link our historical past to our current environmental problems. In Harcourt Brace Jovanovich's *Rise of the American Nation* (1982), a review exercise states, "Pollution of the land and water and misuse of resources began with the first European settlements in America. Explain." The explanation is supposed to include the point that pollution has accompanied development everywhere and is continuing unabated. But with the singular exception of Prentice-Hall's *The United States: A History of the Republic* (1981), there are no meaningful references to the evolution of pollution problems, only blanket condemnations of current practices. In not one instance does a textbook note that:

* Automobile emissions of hydrocarbons, carbon monoxide, and nitrogen oxide are less than half what they were from 1957 to 1967, according to the Council on Environmental Quality.
* The bacteria level in the Hudson River declined by more than 30 percent between 1966 and 1980.
* Lake Erie is now used for swimming, and Lake Michigan for fishing; 15 years ago both were impossible.
* There is more drinking water available now than in the mid-1960s and 50 percent more than in 1961.
* The amount of unhealthy sulfur dioxide in the air has been steadily declining since 1970.
* The unacceptably high levels of carbon monoxide in New York declined from 149 units in 1978 to 63 units in 1983.
* The percent of beneficial dissolved oxygen in New York Harbor increased from 44.4 percent in 1978 to 62.7 percent in 1983.

The major pollution problem in New York in 1890 was horse manure on the streets—a matter said to be responsible for "disease, filth, and thoroughly objectionable conditions in the city." Another turn-of-the century problem was foods systematically adulterated with chemicals; popular concern over this led to the establishment of the Food and Drug Administration in 1924. The recognition of environmental problems didn't begin with the Club of Rome; efforts at remedial action started long before contemporary writers tried to shame us into it.

Recent statements such as the following by Mostafa K. Tolba, executive director of the U.N. Environmental Program (1982), illustrate the extent to which unsubstantiated contentions abound:

> If the nations of the world continue their present policies, they would face by the turn of the century an environmental catastrophe which will witness devastation as complete, as irreversible, as any nuclear holocaust.

see p. 108

This kind of statement should not be allowed to stand unchallenged. It may be reasonable to assume that pollution will accompany modernization in the less-developed sections of the world, as it did in the industrialized West. As nations industrialize there are bound to be new forms of environmental degradation. This is the price one pays for a higher standard of living. In the West pollution often is related to consumer spending—junk heaps, plastic bags, soda cans, abandoned cars. But this picture of a "disposable society" doesn't tell the whole story.

The other part of it is that in the world's wealthy nations there is evidence that hazardous air pollution has been declining for some time. Water quality has improved markedly since 1961 in this country and abroad, despite this claim of the World Future Society: "Before the end of this century, water shortages may have effects as severe as the energy crisis of the 1970's." In the developing nations the proportion of the population served by a safe water supply rose modestly in urban areas and rose markedly among the rural population throughout the 1970s. In the United States, the total number of trees has been increasing, according to the U.S. Department of Agriculture and the Forest Service; wood production (both soft and hard woods) has gone up more than 10 percent since 1952. Arable land has been increasing worldwide, and the land in public parks has gone up 150 percent since 1950 (*Statistical Abstract of the United States, 1980*).

These statistics hardly constitute the "devastation" to which Mr. Tolba refers. Unfortunately it seems that "indoctrination," in this case the promulgation of trendy antigrowth attitudes, takes precedence over instruction in most school textbooks today. Another example of this is the reference to the loss of farmland because of suburbanization. According to the texts, any intrusion on farmland is sacrilege. Scott, Foresman's *People on Earth: A World Geography* (1983) quotes an unspecified source indicating that:

> Every twenty-four hours more than 3,000 acres of green space are lost around this country. Every year this adds up to at least a million acres. . . . [I]ts place is being taken by housing, schools, business, industries, roads, highways. We need these, of course, but not all that are being built.

The phase "we need these" is almost a grudging afterthought; according to the authors, the indisputably abhorrent fact is the loss of farmland. Where, it might be asked, is an explanation of the trade-off between conflicting policy objectives? Is farmland always more desirable than housing tracts? Why isn't it explained that even with the loss of some farmland, crop yields have been continually increasing? Why isn't there some consideration of the relative utility of farm output when there is already overproduction versus the utility of housing units when there is unmet consumer demand?

The economic implications of these decisions are either glossed over or not discussed at all. The textbook authors have a responsibility to explain the concepts of "marginal costs" and "cost-benefit" computations when they analyze environmental issues, as well as the policy alternatives such as "pollution vouchers," which are in effect permits that accept a limited degree of pollution, or calculations of "social cost."

What the textbooks offer is a set of utopian goals: Eliminate pollution, leave the environment pure, and don't tamper with nature. Yet this seemingly straightforward message that purports to recapture—with evangelical verve—the purity of the environment is strangely ambivalent since it also seeks to preserve the material wealth and standard of living that is ostensibly the cause of a great deal of the hated pollution.

Utopian visions are not appropriate guideposts for policymakers. Teachers may not be training policymakers, but neither should they be training dreamers. The teachers' goal should be to cultivate realists who know how to weigh evidence, examine problems, and know how to make informed judgments.

Concern and prudence in dealing with environmental issues is certainly warranted by the potential hazards of the effects of new and unknown chemicals and technologies. But it should be noted—and rarely is—that mankind has already experienced many natural (not man-made) environmental disasters and strains. The human influence is normally more finite, and on a smaller scale, than the impact of natural forces. According to the EPA, the 1981 volcanic eruption on Mount St. Helens caused much more radiation than all the X-ray equipment in the state of Washington. The fear of uncontrolled viral disease through recombinant genetic research can be put into perspective by the realization that there are many examples in nature of spontaneous gene transfer between species. (The many viral infections of bacteria, plants, and animals suggest that the genes of the virus are spliced onto the genes of the host cell on infection and out of the infected cells on release of the virus.) Yet flora and fauna survive. The environment and the ecological system obviously are much more adaptable than some ecological purists would have us believe. Oceans have self-healing qualities, as do forests. If they didn't, so many forms of life would not have been sustained through so many natural disasters.

Maybe at some point in the future we will recognize either exactly how great (and successful) mankind's adaptational skills have been or, alternatively, how reckless we were in tampering with the environment. Some unprecedented catastrophe such as the Black Death may occur, but there is no evidence to suggest this is any more possible now than it once was. For now, all we can say is that the jury is out. We must be prudent; we cannot overstep the bounds of responsible behavior, but we cannot be overcome by inertia, paralyzed by fear, or consumed by the desire to bring back a mythical, pollution-free past. It does make sense to be cautious. According to Environmental Protection Agency estimates, the Delaware River Basin, for example, may have to accommodate a large number of nuclear plants; 32 are projected for the year 2025, which translates into an average of one every nine miles. The Ohio River Valley will be burdened with coal mines and eventually synthetic-fuel plants. The Southwest will have to make water available for mining, thereby lessening the supply for agriculture. Judging from the past, each of these matters will result in a conflict of interests that will be bitter and protracted. No one can project the results or the time frame. But my guess is that the need for jobs, for practical improvements that will benefit consumers, and for profits will be far more compelling than idealistic goals and will ultimately win out. However, as incomes rise and affluence becomes more widespread, a preference for environmental amenities increases accordingly. Here again competing interests will be tested in the area of public opinion and politics.

The environmental issue, in other words, should be used to encourage our students to be critical and to weigh evidence, to recognize the potential benefits and costs of risk-taking. Decision making necessarily entails calculations, compromises, and trade-offs. Dealing with the environment is not a simple matter of right and wrong. That, however, is precisely what one generally finds in the presentation of these issues in the social studies textbooks, and it does neither our students nor our nation any good.

6

Economic Development

The present income disparities between the wealthiest and poorest nations are projected to widen. Assuming that present trends continue . . . industrial countries will have a per capita GNP of nearly $8,500 (in 1975 dollars) in 2000. . . . By contrast, per capita GNP in the LDC's [less-developed countries] will average less than $600. . . .

The Global 2000 Report to the President **(1980)**

For most of the past 20 years, descriptions of economic development have included a stereotype of rich nations benefiting from technology's bounty while poor nations remain impoverished and unaffected by the material advances and increasing wealth of the industrialized world. This "gap" between the "haves" and the "have-nots" is often referred to in U.N. debates and is the major distinction between the "North" and the "South" in a global context. President Carter's Commission for *The Global 2000 Report* emphasized the widening income disparities between rich nations and poor; television commentators and textbooks similarly stress the existence of the gap. Not surprisingly, students across the land have been led to believe that most of the world's people are poor and that only a few privileged ones are prosperous. Charles Elliot, author of *Patterns of Poverty in the Third World* (1975), maintains:

If we believe that the fundamental cause of world poverty is the ability of the privileged to protect and extend their privilege, then we, the rich, need to look very carefully at the structure of our own society.

According to a 1975 Harris survey:

A solid 61-23 percent majority of the American people feels it is morally wrong that Americans, who comprise only 6 percent of the world's population, consume 40 percent of the world's production of energy and raw materials. A 55-30 majority feels that this disparity between population and consumption hurts the well-being of the rest of the world. Consequently, a 50-31 percent plurality is worried that a continuation of this consumption of the world's resources by Americans will turn the rest of the world against us.

We will go back and discuss some of the specifics of these "facts" later, but for now what is important to note is that these statements obscure one of the clearest and most encouraging developments in this century: the emergence of a middle class throughout the world. There are more "middle income" countries than poor ones: A majority of the world's people no longer live in nations where the per-capita income is so low as to be considered poverty level. The gap between rich and poor states certainly has not disappeared, but an exclusive emphasis on the gap is a misleading way to discuss economic development.

Consider a nation with a $500 per-capita income and one with a $4,000 per-capita income. The obvious difference between them is $3,500. Now consider a 100 percent increase in the first instance and a 50 percent increase in the second, leading to per-capita incomes of $1,000 and $6,000, respectively. The poor country would have doubled its per-capita income while the wealthier nation would have experienced half that growth. However, the new gap would indicate an absolute widening of $1,500. This exercise suggests that the relative increases in per-capita income are much more instructive than the nominal values. What should concern us is the progress of the poor, not how they compare to wealthy people elsewhere.

This hypothetical illustration parallels in most significant respects actual cases. For example, Singapore increased its per-capita income from $533 in 1970 to $4,100 in 1980; the United States increased its per-capita income from $3,412 in 1970 to about $8,700 in 1980. The absolute difference between these nations escalated from $2,879 to $4,600, reinforcing the impression of a widening gap. But the more significant reality is that there was an almost 700 percent improvement in Singapore's per-capita G.N.P. while the United States per-capita income improved by only 200 percent. In this instance the "gap" is not nearly as meaningful as the actual improvement in each case.

In another interesting comparison, Japan increased its per-capita G.N.P. from $986 in 1970 to $8,460 in 1980. During the same period, Nigeria's per-capita income went from $63 to $552. In both cases the increase was just under 900 percent. But the income disparity went from $923 to $7,908. Should this illustration suggest that the rich got richer while the poor got poorer? Or should it suggest that both nations made extraordinary and relatively equal economic strides during this period?

In many instances the existence of the gap assists poor nations to accelerate their economic growth. It can motivate nations to catch up. For example, as rich states grow, the demand for resources from poor states increases correspondingly. In addition, as Western industries become knowledge-intensive there are expanding markets for labor-intensive producers in the developing world. This too encourages economic growth. In many ways poor nations benefit from technology transfer, capital investment, and educational opportunities offered by the inflow of Western expertise and resources.

These illustrations demonstrate the existence of a dynamic process of modernization at work. The process is certainly imperfect; not every nation is guaranteed a place on the scale of industrial evolution. But it is appropriate to consider world economic development as a metaphorical frog pond where most tadpoles grow into frogs and some frogs leave the pond. It is, of course, also true that many tadpoles never develop and some die. As an explanation of modernization, the frog pond metaphor is much closer to reality than the black-and-white picture of winners and losers conveyed by the media and our textbooks. Modernization is not a zero-sum game where one side can make gains only at the expense of the other side. The benefits of modernization may not accrue to both sides equally, but they do accrue to both sides.

In an interdependent world economy it is already apparent that the advanced industrialized nations are moving away from producer economies toward service and information industries. As a result, the developing world is becoming increasingly reliant on "smokestack" (heavy, basic) industries. For example, shipbuilding, which was once concentrated in nations such as England, Sweden, and Japan, has shifted to Spain and Brazil; the United States' domination of the manufacturing part of the apparel industry has yielded to Third World countries; even Japan is getting out of steel production by relying instead on its South Korean neighbors. This analysis confirms that there is a comparative advantage for poor nations who find that their low wage rates and abundance of unskilled labor are definite incentives for industrialization. As some advanced industrial nations become heavily involved in knowledge-intensive industries, there are opportunities for developing states to develop capital and labor-intensive industries.

Before I overstate the case, note that there are negative consequences to economic growth. Many important customs associated with traditional values can be undermined by an improvement in material conditions. When life becomes easier, it can lack challenges. Some social critics have argued that affluence has promoted hedonism, drug abuse, and the "sensate" culture. Other maintain that affluence can promote unnecessary and ultimately counterproductive feelings of guilt—the "I have so much and they have so little" syndrome—eventually leading to detrimental antigrowth policies. Although these concerns vary in different cultures, they cannot be underestimated. As Joseph Schumpeter (among others) has noted, these conditions that emanate from economic success often have demoralizing social consequences. His argument suggests that the consequences of success can undermine the conditions needed to promote affluence. For example, recreational drugs may be used by the very wealthy eager for new thrills, but with the consumption of the drugs they lose the drive for success that propelled them to achieve affluence in the first place.

However, it is difficult to consider the fruits of success, much less its negative consequences, when affluence is still a dream. Relatively few people wouldn't risk giving up even some well-established traditions for material well-being. Most ascetics who are willing to renounce material comforts are in the United States, where the notion of self-deprivation is feasible because the risks are so slight.

As David Landes points out in *The Unbound Prometheus* (1969):

There are some in the more advanced industrial countries who have qualms about this worship of material achievement, but they are wealthy and can afford this critical posture. The overwhelming majority of the inhabitants of this world especially the great mass of the hungry and unwashed, take it for granted that food, clothing, and other creature comforts are not only good for both body and soul, but lie within reach.

One of my students stated this issue in another but poignant way: "In this country you can always return to the world of three square meals." For some, their relative poverty is an option they have voluntarily chosen. For most people it is a condition to be overcome in favor of the "materialism" renounced by the ascetics.

In the textbooks, however, the complexity of world economic

conditions and motivations is omitted. One would think from these presentations that world development has remained unchanged since the nineteenth century and that the poor nations are getting poorer and the rich, richer. There is very little suggestion of economic development at the low end of the scale but many suggestions (and explicit citations) that the poor states have not improved their economic condition. What follows are several examples from which a generalization about most textbooks can be drawn:

"A Great Gulf"—Never before in history has there been so wide a gulf between the most advanced peoples and the least. (Silver Burdett, *World Geography,* 1980)

"The Widening Gap"—The gap between rich and poor nations is widening (see graphs). [Note: the graphs do not document the point.] (Houghton, Mifflin, *Unfinished Journey,* 1983)

The world in 1972, economically speaking, was divided in two: a few rich industrial countries and many more poor developing nations. The gap between rich and poor countries was wide. (Macmillan, *Modern Times,* 1983)

The gap between rich and poor countries widened. . . . Some Third World countries were worse off in 1980 than . . . in 1970. (Scott, Foresman, *History and Life: The World and Its People,* 1982)

And the gap between the rich . . . and the poor nations grows wider all the time. (Merrill, *Global Insights: People and Cultures,* 1980)

. . . [T]he gap between the rich, industrial countries and the poor, underdeveloped nations was becoming steadily wider and deeper. (Harcourt Brace Jovanovich, *Rise of the American Nation,* 1977)

. . . split between the developed nations which used so much of the earth's resources and the "underdeveloped" or "developing" nations. (Ginn, *A History of the United States,* 1981)

Both absolutely and relatively, the gap between rich and poor grew wider. (Houghton Mifflin, *The American Economy: Analysis, Issues, Principles,* 1983)

Approximately 130 countries are referred to as developing nations. . . . In spite of the different names used to describe these countries, they all have one thing in common: abject poverty. (Scott, Foresman, *America! America!* 1982)

The developing nations of the world have one thing in common: poverty. . . . [T]he gap between the "have" and the "have nots" becomes even greater each year. (Merrill, *Economics: Principles and Practices,* 1981)

The population explosion has helped increase the gap between rich nations and poor nations. (Prentice-Hall, *World History: Patterns of Civilization,* 1983)

These illustrations do not include comparisons of food consumption that make the same point in another way. Instead they include examples in which the poor in ancient cultures are compared with wealthy states today (for example, Silver Burdett,

This Is Our World, 1981), an illustration that smacks of the apples-and-oranges comparison.

Related to the issue of the "gap" in the textbook presentations is the nearly universal omission of an obvious point: What we now call a "poor nation" was the universal condition for all states 200 years ago. Until the industrial revolution, "poor" was natural and unexceptional. By contemporary standards even the rich nations of the nineteenth century appear poor. Simple designations of "rich" and "poor" minimize much of the world's economic diversity. Rich nations have poor people, and poor nations include rich ones. The poor people in rich nations are aware of the wealth around them, but it does them no good to be grouped into the category of a wealthy nation.

A sound perspective on rich and poor becomes even more complicated when purchasing-power parity is considered. Buying the same pair of shoes in India and France will result in different purchase prices. The only way to measure the impact of the purchase is to compare the number of work hours required to buy the shoes. For example, the price of the shoes—if domestically produced—in a poor country will include the relatively low labor cost and perhaps the low expense for materials. The essential question is what portion of someone's income it takes to buy those shoes, or how many hours of work (translated into its compensation) is needed to obtain the shoes. This issue was addressed in only one of the texts examined, Houghton Mifflin's *The American Economy* (1983). What we read usually is that Indians (of all classes) are necessarily worse off than the French—a conclusion that would be startling to the upper class of India and the lower class of France. But this misleading picture is bound to emerge as long as textbook writers rely more on a Manichean conception of economic development than on a continuum or spectrum of relative conditions.

However, the emotional impact of the textbook arguments would be lost if clear divisions of black and white became shades of gray.

In Globe's *The New Exploring: A Changing World* (1980), the emotional appeal and effort to evince guilt are well dramatized in an extended quotation from a book written by Robert Heilbroner in 1963. In this statement he attempts to describe how Americans should view poverty in the underdeveloped world:

> . . . how a typical American family . . . could be transformed into an equally typical family of the underdeveloped world. . . . Everything goes: beds, chairs, table, television set, lamps. . . . We will permit a pair of shoes to the head of the family, but none for the wife or children. . . . The box of matches may stay, a small bag of flour, some sugar and salt. A few mouldy potatoes, already in the garbage can, must be hastily rescued, for they will provide much of tonight's meal.
>
> Now we take away the house. The family can move to the toolshed. . . . And still we have not reduced our American family to the level at which life is lived in the greatest part of the globe.

In another section of this text a black man is shown washing a car. The caption reads: "In Africa today, Western comforts are part of the daily life of many. How many problems result when people try to combine their traditional ways with the ways of Western countries?" This is the proverbial double bind. If Africans develop their economy in an effort to close "the gap," then they jeopardize their traditional ways; if they maintain the status quo and preserve their traditional ways, they can't close "the gap." Damned if you do, damned if you don't. As I've already noted, modernization invariably entails cultural and social changes. If you don't want the change, then you shouldn't lament economic problems. Textbook authors, however, seem to want it both ways. That isn't only faulty reasoning, it is simply unrealistic.

Silver Burdett's *World Geography* (1980) follows this same path to emotional despair with this epigrammatic inquiry: "These two societies, the developed and the developing, live side by side on this earth. How long can this gulf continue to exist between them?" What are students supposed to do with the emotions aroused by these rhetorical questions?

Scott, Foresman's *History and Life: The World and Its People* (1982) asks, "Why did the gap between rich and poor countries grow wider?" and answers the question in the teacher guide with the statement: "As the wealthy countries grew richer at an increasingly faster pace, the gap between them and the Third World widened." What should have been said (here and elsewhere) is that in recent history the rich get richer and the poor get richer. This point of view, however, doesn't square with the apparent neo-Calvinism of textbook writers.

It also explains why the statement "The United States, with only 6 percent of the world's population, uses 40 percent of the world's resources" appears with regularity in most of the textbooks. It could easily be mentioned—and rarely is—that the United States also accounts for 40 percent of the world's production and that it is indefensible to suggest that Americans live well at the expense of other nations. In fact, a case could be made for the position that people in many lands would live less well, and many would starve, if the United States were not as productive as it is. Instead, the textbook profile of economic development, whether described through statistics or narrative, suggests that there are unfortunate economic conditions in the world for which we are responsible and should be ashamed. The message students are getting is, "You've got to do something about this deplorable situation."

Textbook publishers have an obligation to create a reasonable perspective on economic issues, not to create feelings of guilt. As Daniel Bell notes in the *Post-Industrial Society*, the world economy has moved from primary production (extractive) to secondary (productive) and tertiary (service and information processing) and is now heading toward quaternary production ("doing things for their own sake"). Surely this transition has not been completed, but the first three stages are quite discernible. Anyone who can recall how his great-grandparents and grandparents lived is aware of the progress that has accompanied these stages of development. Until my children were taken to a farm, they believed that chickens came out of a supermarket freezer. They had no conception of primary production. Moreover, the process of slaughtering and packaging these chickens was also unknown to them. It simply was taken for granted. Only at the tertiary stage—the marketing of the product—do they confront a "chicken." But now it is nicely wrapped, its feathers are removed, its parts may be cut, and it is frozen solid. It resembles a plastic art object more than a former animal. Conceivably even the tertiary stage can be shortened when one does "computer shopping" and the frozen bird is delivered to your door. At that point my grandchildren probably will believe that chickens appear miraculously at one's doorstep ready for consumption, a product of providential will like manna from heaven.

These changes have positive implications, but they also cause problems. In taking everything for granted, one can easily lose appreciation for what one has. How can you appreciate the conditions necessary for chicken farming, when you never see a live chicken and don't see chickens slaughtered so you can have food to eat? How can one decide about material conditions when one's experience is so limited? Economist Thorstein Veblen discussed "trained incapacity" as afflicting highly educated children of affluence who are so removed from practical "real world" experiences that they are virtually trained to be incapable of performing or understanding basic routine daily functions. The concept of technologically revolutionized chicken farming may be comprehensible to them; a live and squawking chicken isn't.

Then there are those problems I would put under the category of boredom (world-weariness is the popular expression). This could be an affliction resulting from having whatever material things one wants; the search then turns instead to the "heightened experience." Steven Marcus described this unfolding condition quite aptly as "pornucopia." There is a marvelous scene in *La Dolce Vita* that makes this point: Marcello Mastroianni is walking down a dark Roman street with a beautiful woman hanging on each arm. His suit is white and magnificently tailored. His white hat is worn on the side with panache, and he swaggers confidently like a man who has "everything." As he continues walking, two shirtless workmen with pickaxes in their hands enviously watch his every movement. Sweat is pouring off their brows; their hands and faces are filthy. When Mastroianni passes they shake their heads as if to say, "Why can't that be me?" At that moment Mastroianni says to his companions, "Oh, how I wish I, too, had meaning in my life." The man with "everything" longs to be the street laborer. This could well turn out to be the appropriate metaphor for the "new class" (the upper-middle class composed of scholars, journalists, lawyers, and assorted intellectuals who work with "symbols" rather than physical problems) as it enters the postindustrial society.

Some will regard postindustrial society as stagnant, incapable of marshaling the drive that propels economic development. Some will argue that societies without smokestack industries are "effete," that the production of steel and automobiles keeps a nation strong and "manly." But the evolution is already under way, and much of the transition is completed. Those who report on history have a duty to describe where we've come from and to speculate on where this economic development will take us. Part of that duty is to be able to be as objective as possible.

It is fashionable to be pessimistic and to decry accomplishments. But textbook writers have a responsibility to transcend the present mood. They should appraise our history accurately and cite problems when that is appropriate and achievements when they are real. But more than anything else, these educators should attempt to teach, not preach. That translates into presenting a variety of viewpoints with background material to buttress arguments. Anything less than that lowers the standards of appropriate research and teaching. Yet emotional and unsubstantiated offerings, I am sorry to report, are what most textbooks now call "economic analysis."

7

Outlook on the Future

We are entering a new age of man. . . . [O]nly Consciousness III can make possible the continued survival of man as a species in this age of technology. . . .

Charles Reich, *The Greening of America* (1970)

W hether Charles Reich's Consciousness III is a big con or not, there is something to his assertion that we are entering "a new age of man." Of course, Reich isn't the first and certainly won't be the last to say so— there always have been and always will be those who speculate about the future. From Nostradamus to Alvin Toffler, people have predicted the way in which things will turn out. This is seemingly a benign activity—a little like examining our horoscope to determine our daily fate. Actually, that isn't the case at all.

In speculating about the future we attempt to shape the course of events so that what we are told to expect, what we would like to happen, and what is probable all converge. Our vision of the future, therefore, helps to bring it about. In *The Origin and Goal of History* (1953), Karl Jaspers wrote:

No prognosis is harmless. Whether it is true or untrue, it ceases to be a contemplative vision and becomes a call to action. What man deems possible moves his inner attitude and his deeds. To see the dangers with just concern is a precondition for his self-assertion, whereas illusionary notions and obfuscations drag him into ruin.

One would think that most students and authors are initially agnostic about the future. A viewpoint develops when one studies social behavior, economic shifts, technological developments, and political organization. But this viewpoint isn't dispassionate. Wittingly or unwittingly, a view of the future affects actions, attitudes, and morale in the present so that one has an obligation to describe problems that seem intractable (to deal with them), those for which there are likely solutions (to find remedies), and those uncertainties and matters of great potential and promise that lie ahead (to excite and motivate our energies).

For example, are scientific developments likely to be beneficial or problematical? How can we know? How have scientific discoveries in the past affected society? What breakthroughs are on the horizon? What are the consequences of these changes? Surely there are no surprise-free scenarios, but there are ways of making reasonable assumptions about the future. What lies ahead may not be entirely clear, but it is not at all useful to describe it as unknowable.

There is widespread agreement today that five technologies will shape our immediate and perhaps medium-term future: computers, cybernation, space colonies, energy alternatives, and communications. By being aware of these technologies we can create a framework for discussion. A space colony, for example, may be conceived of as a new living space unlike anything experienced heretofore, or as the mirroring and extension of Earth settlements. It can be an opportunity for experimentation or an expansion of what already exists. But this new technology—by its very existence—encourages discussion and speculation. This is not a value-free exercise; it considers the possibilities from the Golden Age to the Brave New World with the permutations in between.

However, most textbook considerations of the future seem not to want to educate and stimulate debate. Rather, they seem intent on encouraging pessimism. One finds an emphasis on problems rather than opportunities. In part this is due to the misleading treatment of population and food, resources, environment, and economic development issues. Certainly there are exceptions to the pervasive pessimism, but the exceptions are generally afterthoughts presented as unsupported generalities. It's somewhat like saying, "We are going to hell in a handbasket, but there's always hope." Or Franz Kafka's variation on this theme, "There is always hope, but not for us."

Scott, Foresman's *Living World History* (1982) establishes a contrast between "some social critics in the West" who argue against equating continued industrialization with progress and "leaders in the developing countries" who see industrialization as "the best hope of eliminating crushing poverty." This insight is useful (and refreshing). But economic development for developing states is considered appropriate at all times by most textbook authors; while for the industrialized West, economic development always is considered selfish and even hazardous. Why are the criteria so different?

In discussing economic development in the West, the argument is also made that the transfer of technology is more difficult now than it used to be. Macmillan's *Global Geography* (1981) contends that technological innovations today are more complex than when immigrants to the New World memorized the blueprints for textile machinery. In addition, this text argues, "starting a business is much more difficult and expensive" than was true in the past. Not only are these two conclusions "downers" in that they tend to dampen any entrepreneurial spirit, they also point to a future of restricted opportunity that is quite contrary to actual conditions. If, for example, the demographics in the state of Florida in 1983 provide a reasonable basis for projecting the demographics of this nation circa 2000 (average age about 45), every 10-year-old today will find himself in the unique position of being able to start a business before he's 30 years old. Opportunities in the employment force will be bountiful, a situation that isn't restricted to the United States, since large sections of the globe (for example, Western Europe) are "graying" more quickly than we are.

A few textbooks emulate Draper Kauffman's teacher guide to future studies (*Futurism and Future Studies*) in suggesting that it would be beneficial for poor countries if the rich ones would stop growing. As I suggested in Chapter 6, economic development in the developing world is dependent on the achievements of the developed world. If the latter is depressed, who will buy the former's products? If the developed nations lose their wealth, where will the developing world obtain its credits and loans? Whether we like it or not, the world is economically interdependent. The success of one area depends on the success of another, just as failure in one area can have devastating effects in other parts of the world.

Fortunately, the foolish idea that growth in the industrial world has to stop to give developing countries a chance to catch up is not explicitly supported by most textbook publishers. However, it is common to suggest a relationship between rich nations consuming less and poor nations having more. Very often this relationship is presented through a discussion of foreign aid. Harcourt Brace Jovanovich's *Rise of the American Nation* (1977), for example, describes the rich-poor "gap" as having reached "crisis proportions" and notes that "the rich, industrial nations would have to carry a major share of the responsibility for alleviating the problems of poverty and hunger in the world" through economic assistance. The political and economic difficulties associated with foreign aid, the corruption and lassitude it can promote, and the way it sometimes inhibits productivity (in addition to the reluctance of some nations even to accept it) are not part of these discussions.

For example, Tanzania's President Julius K. Nyerere, whose country is a much-favored recipient of foreign aid, has used these funds to move millions of people forcibly into socialist camps, often far from their native villages. The upshot of this policy has been a dramatic decline in food production. Zaïre's President Mobuto Sese Seko, whose nation is another recipient of extensive foreign aid, has expelled large numbers of foreign traders only to find that this has resulted in subsistence production over large areas of his country, causing widespread deprivation and hardship. As P. T. Bauer in *Equality, the Third World and Economic Development* (1981) pointed out, foreign aid has created two myths: that there is a collectivity of nations with common interests called the Third World and that the West is a collectivity of homogeneous states manipulating the world economy to its own advantage. If one accepts the second idea, there is the likelihood that the notion of aid to these developing states will be seen as a "moral imperative." As Bauer and Melvyn Krass in *Development Without Aid* (1983) have suggested, aid generally increases the money, patronage, and power of recipient governments. It can promote a politicization of life that translates into reliance on bureaucratic and administrative decisions, diverting energy and resources from productive activity. Although one may not necessarily agree with this viewpoint, not one text includes the idea of development without aid—that is, the use of nonmaterial incentives such as technical equipment, information transfer, and tax incentives as catalysts for economic development.

Laidlaw's *A History of Our American Republic* (1981) is a prototypical example of how textbooks deal with the matter of future economic growth. It is discussed as a "mixed blessing," albeit praise is heaped on slower growth because it will reduce pollution, conserve resources, and save the environment. The textbook summary makes the point:

> The United States is a post-industrial country. But it is not certain that the economy will keep growing. If it does, a major question in the future will be whether continued growth will be good for the country.

This is a defensible position. But it serves primarily as propaganda if stated without substantive opposition. I would like to see a follow-up paragraph stating both the positive and negative potential of continued growth, or else a disclaimer of the kind presented in Harcourt Brace Jovanovich's *The Development of American Economic Life* (1978), which prefaces its antigrowth argument with this statement: "Warning: This will not be a 'balanced' view of life in the United States today."

Perhaps the most extreme version of the future is presented in Allyn & Bacon's *The Pageant of American History*, published in 1975 and mercifully going out of print. The ostensible goal of this text is to translate a message on the environment into fear and anxiety. The general statement "The earth's resources may have reached their limit to provide for human beings. The destruction of our environment, moreover, is closely related to the population problem" is used as prologue for a quotation from J. C. Mitchell and C. L. Stallings (eds.), *Ecotactics: The Sierra Club Handbook for Environment Activists* (1970):

About every four seconds, the United States census clock ticks off a new American. In his expected 70 years of life, he will contribute to the Gross National Product by consuming 50 tons of food, 28 tons of iron and steel, 1,200 barrels of petroleum products, a ton and a half of fiber and 4,500 cubic feet of wood and paper. All of this material will pass through or around the new American, eventually winding up as waste—100 tons of it, wafting on the breeze, bobbing in mid-current, or along with his "10,000 no deposit, no return" bottles, ploughed into some hapless marsh, there to pollute both the land and the sea.

136

The section concludes with this inquiry: "Do we need to be destroyed before we can be reborn?"

Another text, Ginn's *A History of the United States* (1981), uses a series of rhetorical questions that both lament the past and worry about the future in order to ask how we are going to survive technical advances.

Who would have guessed that, within less than 200 years, a trackless, half-mapped continent could be crisscrossed by superhighways, defaced by billboards and tin cans? Who would have guessed that Americans would perfect horseless carriages to go a hundred miles an hour—and yet be stuck in traffic jams. . .? Or that ten times as many would be killed by these horseless carriages every year as were killed in all the battles of the American Revolution?

Who would have imagined that the fresh air of a New World would begin to be smoke-filled? Or that the sparkling waters of lakes and rivers would become so darkened and dirtied by factory sewage that even the fish found them un-livable . . .?

Who would have believed that the wonderful American silences . . . would be shattered by the roar of speeding jets, lumbering trucks, and ear-jarring motorcycles? Who would have believed that a continent, once frightening by its emptiness, would now terrify people by crowding them together?

Who would have foreseen that a nation rich in natural resources—in coal, oil, uranium, natural gas, and flowing water—would fear that it might be crippled by a lack of enough energy to run its cars and factories and to warm its . houses?

Harcourt Brace Jovanovich's *The Development of American Economic Life* (1978) makes the same point by asking: "Industrial America is certainly richer than colonial America. Are we sure that it is also better and happier?" If one were to extend this argument, the next edition of the textbook may well suggest, "Postindustrial America is richer than industrial America, but is it better and happier?"

Many imponderables are associated with technological development, but there also are extraordinary opportunities. What is not clear is the reason for the almost total omission in our textbooks of the promise of technology; one finds instead an overwhelming preponderance of prognostications of fear and doom. Certainly fear is a powerful motivator and has already had some influence in reducing energy consumption and making Americans conscious that they must learn to be responsible about their environment. But fear is no replacement for high morale, sustained by confidence in the possibility of real achievement. That is the real catalyst for positive change.

Those textbook authors who use doomsday visions to promote "virtuous behavior" contribute to a weakening of the national consensus needed for meaningful action. How can men and women devote themselves to future-oriented actions of any kind if they aren't confident there will be a future? How can one remain loyal to this nation when its past triumphs are described as deleterious? How optimistically can we plan ahead when we are told to assume the future will necessarily be worse than the past? Every previous generation in American history believed its children would be better off than it is; today, youngsters are taught that their children will not live nearly as well or as healthfully as they do.

The current crisis of declining output and production in Western societies is an expression of the social and cultural disruption caused by this kind of negative orientation. It's not a crisis fostered by technological advances but one of the spirit in which the ethos of consumption has produced a generation that takes for granted the fruits of productivity. It is, perhaps, a condition that will turn out to be endemic to affluent, technically advanced nations. Perhaps, then, this economic, attitudinal downtrend is the fate of a postindustrial society.

But the future can be influenced by the belief that human effort can change the course of events. There is little doubt that morale will play a role in the kind of future we create as well as in our perspective toward our further technical advances. If we believe that through our ingenuity and determination we can shape the society we wish to have, it is likely to happen. This perspective is very much like that of William James, who also argued for "a belief in potency," in the power of individual belief and confidence to affect the unfolding of future events. Detractors might suggest that such faith may well be a necessary but insufficient factor in shaping the future. I would agree. Will does not triumph in isolation. The future will depend on technology, capital, and human resources. But they too are insufficient without human will.

It may be the role of teachers and textbook authors to promote positive morale about the future. It is certainly *not* their role to encourage pessimism. In an effort to be objective and realistic, both the problems and the promise of the future should be presented. One way this can be done is by considering the ways in which previous societies dealt with their prospects. Fred Polak in *Images of the Future* (1976) said:

Either the emptiness of utopian and eschatological images of the future will mean the emptiness and maybe the end of Western culture, or there will be a new spiritual soul searching for meaningful and magnetizing images of the future.

The point, of course, is that the dramatic choices he cites are our choices. It is not enough to say we are on the threshold of some spectacular change. This turning point in history may be the moment when civilization is crushed, as Pierre Teilhard de Chardin writes, or the era in which mankind can "laugh and reach out their hands amidst the stars," as H. G. Wells predicted. But it makes no sense to paint a future of horrors. It is a distinct disservice to students to describe technology as our enemy, as the new Frankenstein monster uncontrolled. To argue—as many texts do—that people are disillusioned with technology because it won't deliver utopia is like arguing that antiseptics ought to be banned because pharmaceutical companies can't assure immortality.

Textbook authors and publishers who take delight in a future world of diminished expectations may be helping to create a world without a textbook market too. But if the history of the past 200 years is any guide to the future, their extreme claims will be part of history's detritus, for mankind, unhampered by ideology, is likely to enlarge its dominion over nature and increase the abundance that nature reluctantly yields. Abundance is not a natural condition, scarcity is. That is something students should learn not only to improve their morale but also to prepare them to understand their future. Until the twentieth century, poverty was the general condition of mankind; relative affluence is a new feature of modern life. In fact, it can be argued that a secretary in 1983 lives better than a nobleman in 1800. She has hot and cold running water in her apartment, indoor toilets, electricity, two or three weeks' vacation, and home entertainment in the form of a television set. She has probably traveled across the country or to Europe, she can travel distances on a daily commute that a nobleman in 1800 would have considered a week's voyage. She has electric conveniences at home and on the job of which a nineteenth-century nobleman never dreamed. She probably can cool her home or office in summer and heat it in winter. She can commune with nature in a national park or escape from nature's hazards in a comfortable apartment. Most importantly, technology has given her security and mobility unknown to her ancestors.

Textbooks, on the other hand, mythologize nature as eternally serene and benign until disturbed by man. When mankind doesn't interfere, there is a mystical harmony and romance. Rarely are we reminded that nature contains volcanoes belching radiation into the atmosphere, floods that overwhelm river towns, tornadoes that lift unsuspecting people to oblivion, and many other lethal or life-threatening conditions too numerous to specify here. This is the very nature we have been relatively successful in subduing. Mankind's greatest accomplishment has been in harnessing many of nature's proclivities and thereby creating civilization. Yet if one were to take seriously the claims in the texts, we would turn our clock back to a pristine wilderness where people were entirely at the mercy of natural forces. Certainly serious authors recognize the absurdity of this position, but in their eagerness to criticize the excesses of technology, textbook writers often overlook the violence in nature and the dangers to mankind.

The prevailing opinion of the future is one-dimensional. It is a future fraught with hazards. A natural response to this would be to hide one's head, ostrichlike, in the sand. However, neither the response nor the dismal characterization of the future is appropriate or accurate. Our outlook should be mixed—hopeful and cautious—and allow for calculated risks while exhibiting guarded concern for one's personal and geographical environment. To retreat from the future is impossible. The test of our mettle is how effectively we can influence it to bring about desired results—for example, increased health and safety, expanded economic opportunities. The test for educators is to prepare students well to address future challenges.

Textbook publishers have a responsibility to prepare students by giving them the best information available from which to develop an accurate analysis of the present and a reasonable scenario of the future. What we have instead is a textbook future of hazards, problems, and "mine fields" and a conception of technology that is uninspiring at best and terrifying at worst.

8

Limits to Growth Ideology

The most developed nations are on the way toward a breakdown on a large scale.
Roberto Vacca, *The Coming Dark Age* (1973)

F or some time a feeling of malaise has been present in this
nation. It is pervasive and constant, although it waxes and
wanes on specific events. For example, the time the hostages
were taken and held in Iran was a moment of national depres-
sion; the day of their release was a time for exhilaration. Similarly, each successful space shot temporarily overshadows
national woe, but the feeling of malaise doesn't go away. Literature of the past decade confirms this mood.

Robert Heilbroner in *An Inquiry into the Human Prospect*
(1974) writes:

The answer to whether we can conceive of the future other
than as a continuation of the darkness, cruelty, and disorder
of the past seems to me to be no; and to the question whether
worse impends, yes.

Paul and Anne Ehrlich in *The End of Affluence* (1974)
maintain:

We are facing, within the next three decades, the disintegra-
tion of an unstable world of nation states infected with
growthmania.

Dennis Meadows in *Business Week* (1975) argues:

The material standard of living will have declined sufficiently
by the end of the 1980s to pull the rug out from under a lot of
consumer mass markets. I think it's likely that the U.S. economy is going to deteriorate very seriously.

F. A. Cotter in *Science* (1975) tells us:

We have systematically, in the name of humaneness, eliminated nearly all of nature's checks and balances on the human
population, and in so doing, we have moved very far in the
direction of creating a hell on earth of our design.

Robert Theobold in *Beyond Despair* (1976) contends:

We still do not understand that the ways we think and the
decision-making patterns we use prevent us from coming to
grips with the continuing breakdown of our socioeconomic
system and our culture.

Theodore Caplow et al. in *Middletown Families* (1982)
conclude:

With respect to the larger society, Middletown is gloomy
indeed. What people of all ages see as they look into the
future is nuclear war, environmental deterioration of the
quality of life. . . . The alternative to catastrophe that they
desire is not continued progress but a prolongation of the
status quo.

These allegations are reinforced by media presentations that
tell us we will soon run out of drinking water, topsoil, and clean
air (the topics of three television network specials aired in
1983). This mood is greatly enhanced by real events. Vietnam,
urban riots, assassinations, Watergate, Three Mile Island,
Abscam, inflation, nuclear weapons, and crime are some of the
pegs that symbolize increasing public apprehension since 1965.
As the Harris surveys since 1966 illustrate, there is a trend
toward decreasing confidence in our major institutions—for
example, large corporations, the military, the medical profes-

sion, colleges, religion, the U.S. Supreme Court, the press, organized labor, Congress, the Executive branch. Similarly, the sense of optimism that historians once considered a central characteristic of American life has been declining since the mid-1950s, as documented by a variety of polls conducted by Daniel Yankelovich and *Fortune* magazine. It is no coincidence that in the late 1970s Daniel Bell wrote an article titled "The End of American Exceptionalism."

It is, of course, also no surprise that an affluent nation would spawn an elite that exhibits a disdain for materialism and chooses instead a simple and aesthetically congenial way of life. Anxiety about unlimited economic growth as well as a distaste for the unpleasant features of suburban sprawl, traffic jams, overcrowding, congestion, and so on, are characteristic of this mind-set. Anitra Thorhaug in a Club of Rome-sponsored publication, *Making It Happen: A Positive Guide to the Future* (1982), argues:

> Paving the land for shopping centers, highways, and creeping suburbs must halt. Our cities must expand upward, not outward. The land is not only vital for food production but for maintenance of a viable global ecosystem of water, air, soil, and soil minerals, on which we and our companion species depend.

Stewart Udall, commenting on the energy crisis of 1973, said, "In terms of urban policy, this is good news. It means sprawl is over." This point of view usually is asserted as a concern for environmental protection. Very often that concern is genuine. Sometimes, however, it represents the attitude of an elite that is selfishly worried about the intrusion of the masses onto its isolated fishing streams or remote beaches. Often it represents the will of an intelligentsia skeptical about the fruits of economic progress.

But there is something else at stake in this antigrowth position— it is the implicit declaration that we have reached the end of abundance, that our nation no longer can strive for material progress, that we must limit our vision. That notion explains why there is so much interest in the redistribution (via welfare, food stamps, Social Security, etc.) of existing wealth. It explains why equality is the clarion call of these times, not individualism. But the problem with these arguments is in determining who does the redistribution for whom. What is meant by economic "fairness"? Is it each according to his needs, or each according to his contribution? What constitutes need? How does one evaluate a worthwhile contribution? No society can keep individual freedom intact when these judgments must be made. The price of redistribution is ultimately some form of expanded government authority and some loss of personal freedom.

Textbooks tend to reflect this elitist attitude and reinforce this social trend away from personal responsibility. Their authors are products of the same milieu that produced songs such as "Stand or Fall" by the Fixx, which portrays the end of the world with "empty faces that describe extinction." What has evolved is a "limits to growth" ideology based on the syllogism that growth cannot continue indefinitely; that the time for "doubling" becomes even shorter; and that there must be an end to this folly to avert a catastrophe. The perspective is well summarized in Merrill's *Economics: Principles and Practices* (1981):

In 1973, a prestigious international group of scholars and business people called the Club of Rome startled the world with a doomsday statement. They warned that global catastrophe would result if nations continued at a steady rate of growth with disregard for levels of population, resources, and pollution. . . .The Club of Rome's theory shook the world. . . . Much discussion ensued on how to bring about zero population growth and zero economic growth. However, the view of the future with little or no economic growth was a dismal one. . . . Slowly, a new and more helpful consensus has evolved around the concept of "organic growth." The benefits of science and technology are to be used to improve the quality of life, but to avoid pollution and conserve resources that can never be renewed. While this seems a happy prospect, there remains a serious question as to whether it can become reality.

In the same year Prentice-Hall published *The Economic Problem* by Robert L. Heilbroner and Lester C. Thurow, a book that deals with the issue in a somewhat different way:

Our standard of living can be maintained, at least for a while. But no one any longer takes for granted that we can continue to race into the future on the path of exponential, self-fueling growth. . . . [T]he energy situation arises from the barriers that all such systems must sooner or later face: Either they will outpace the ability of their resources to sustain their growth or they will bump into barriers of pollution or ecological danger generated by their mushrooming growth. The energy squeeze is the first serious brush that our expanding industrial system has encountered with these constraints of nature. Even if enormous new energy sources are discovered, it is unlikely that our growth trajectory could be sustained more than another generation or two. Our industrial processes are already threatening the environment. . . . Perhaps the most serious threat is the "greenhouse effect" that results from the continuously growing addition of carbon dioxide to the atmosphere as a by-product of energy use. . . . The National Academy of Sciences has warned that we must throttle back on combustion if we are not to disturb the earth's climate.

The "greenhouse effect" to which the authors refer is caused not so much from "combustion" in general as from the combustion of fossil fuels in particular, which does increase the amount of carbon dioxide in the air. If the effect is "the most serious threat" we face, a concerted effort to cope with this threat to our environment would mean solving the problems associated with the generation of nuclear power, which is clean, and the manufacture of synthetic fuels that are low in carbon content. But Heilbroner and Thurow don't make this point, nor does any other textbook that includes this issue.

The ideologists tend to emphasize the growth in population and the increasing pace of worldwide industrialization since 1945 and the accompanying problems they have created. Usually excluded from this picture is any mention of the improvement in the general standard of living, and the emergence of a middle class in the less-developed nations—something that was scarcely imaginable at the end of World War II. In their scenario of the future, most of these ideologically oriented textbook authors cite continued, unplanned growth followed by stagnation and collapse. This bleak picture, they tell us, will result from either the depletion of mineral reserves or pollution caused by industrial production, or some combination of the two. E. F. Schumacher is not a textbook writer, but his sentiments have had a powerful hold on those authors who seemingly take their inspiration from such comments as the following in *Small Is Beautiful:*

In the excitement over the unfolding of his scientific and

technical powers, modern man has built a system of production that ravishes nature and a type of society that mutilates man.

This system of production can cause major problems and has the potential to result in disasters—perhaps major ones—but the impression of mankind hurtling itself blindly to the brink of irreparable damage is not a reasonable or responsible scenario. Although technology can increase the hazards of living, its ostensible purpose is to enhance life's conditions. The idea of technology being created to mutilate man is a figment of Schumacher's well-developed imagination. Curiously, sometimes the avowed environmentalist is drawn to disaster. Steward Brand, creator of *The Whole Earth Catalogue,* is quoted in *Next* magazine (November/December 1980) as having said:

> We have wished, we ecofreaks, for a disaster, or for dramatic social change to come and bomb us into the Stone Age, where we might live like Indians in our valley, with our localism, our Appropriate Technology, our gardens and our homemade religion, guilt-free at last.

Several textbooks dwell on the theme of global violence brought about by teeming numbers and frustrated expectations, while others, such as Laidlaw's *A History of Our American Republic* (1981), rely on the United Nations' rhetoric of an emerging "new world order" built on the large populations and massive resources of the developing states. The dominant theme in both, and in other texts that stress an ideological view, is the "limits to growth" argument wedded to the existence of the disparity between rich and poor nations—"the gap." This view of the world suggests that further industrialization will be harmful to the environment and then portrays an inert mass of victims in the developing world facing deprivation due to "greedy" Western technology. It seems to suggest that we should be responsible for these people in the developing nations who are incapable of taking care of themselves. One geography text confirms the point by entitling its last chapter, "Supporting the World's Developing Nations."

The stereotype drawn in many of these texts depicts the developing world as composed of nations that are merely pawns in historical evolution, populations of mindless breeders and indigenes who have been forced out of their traditional ways by insensitive Western industrialists. Rarely are the achievements of these countries acknowledged (or the enormous improvements brought about with the help of these insensitive Westerners). In not one text is the extension of life expectancy celebrated, yet in the aggregate, the developing states have witnessed a 50 percent increase in median life-span since the end of World War II. In not one text is there a rational explanation for high fertility in these countries, yet it is well established that as long as infant mortality rates were so high the demand for many children was inescapable. As infant mortality rates have declined, so has the birth rate. None of the texts points out that not all trade with the developing world is advantageous to the West; there are numerous examples of countries that have received loans and trade credits and now can't pay even the interest on the debt, much less the principal. And not one text makes the point that it isn't only affluent Americans (or Europeans) who threaten the environment and traditional life-styles of the populations in developing countries; the wanton killing of elephants in Kenya for their ivory, to cite one example, occurred without Western support.

Almost half (31) of the texts reviewed mentioned catastrophic possibilities for the future in developing and developed nations alike. These disasters usually are presented as resulting from the malevolent human impact on the delicate balance in nature. The image, to use the language of one text, is one of "a rundown earth with a runaway population." Macmillan's *Global Geography* (1981) notes, "The earth . . . has built-in controls which help regulate heat. But what happens when human beings interfere with these controls?"

It is also part of the general ideology to assert that it is not possible to make a technological change without upsetting the natural balance. The idea that even minor technical changes can have unanticipated negative effects owes its origin to Garrett Hardin. This argument may be true in part, but only in part. A technical change may affect the social context in which it was spawned, but one can't automatically draw the inference— which ideologists do—that any change is automatically harmful. The history of technology is filled with examples of relatively limited innovations having unexpected, significant applications. For example, Eli Whitney's invention of interchangeable parts for guns led to mass production; research into an ulcer drug led to the creation of soft drinks sweetened without sugar or saccharine. Yet this perspective of unanticipated positive results is routinely excluded from the textbooks.

It is instructive to consider how the texts deal with the "Green Revolution," the scientific breakthroughs that have brought about amazing increases in crop yields. Instead of using this as an example of how science can be usefully applied to problems of world hunger, the undesirable side effects of this revolutionary process usually are emphasized to the exclusion of anything else. For example, Harcourt Brace Jovanovich's *Men and Nations: A World History* (1975) states: "Many new developments offered both threats and promises. The green revolution promised to help relieve the threat of widespread famine; its need for chemical fertilizer threatened the environment." It is, of course, worth asking if the (small) threat isn't worth the (significant) benefit. That analysis, however, isn't included. Similarly, when Rand McNally's *The Promise of Democracy: The Grand Experiment* (1978) discusses food supplies in this country, it flatly condemns the fact that three-fourths of the nation's grain is fed to livestock. "Much of it could be processed into grain for human consumption. If this were done, the world food supply would be increased by at least 30 percent." At no point do the authors suggest that this nation must have reached an extraordinary stage of development to have adopted this practice and at the same time virtually to have eliminated starvation and to have vast quantities of grain left over to export for famine relief.

It is interesting that only one textbook mentions the relationship between limits to growth and negative economic consequences. What one usually finds is the suggestion that changes in values and life-styles are brought about solely through choices; there is no recognition that there may be a causal link between limits to growth policies and a reduction in affluence. If a nation decides that a "limit to growth" should be established, its government can take those steps to curtail economic development. But once this decision is made, the standard of living for most people in that nation cannot improve. If policies are enacted to redistribute money, the incentives for the creation of new wealth will be greatly diminished.

However, when cause-and-effect relationships are mentioned in the textbooks it is usually to account for pernicious results— an increase in population is eventually reflected in food shortages; continued use of minerals at present levels presumably leads to resource depletion. Only when discussing global interdependence are causal relationships viewed as desirable: For example, Globe's *Exploring World History* (1983) concludes with a chapter entitled, "A World of Connections Between People" in which connections are seen as a backdrop for cultural harmony. Certainly one can't quarrel with the ideal of harmony, but what is uniformly excluded from these "interdependence" scenarios are the monetary problems caused by interdependence, and the difficulties in satisfying military procurement needs when global dependency is the goal. How can a banking system (for example, the International Monetary Fund) continue to provide capital for investments in the developing world if its loans are not repaid? How does a small nation mobilize for a limited conventional or guerrilla war when many of its defense needs are being met by another state that doesn't sense the urgency of the internal or local event?

In most of the textbooks global disharmony is depicted through a caricature of rich nations gobbling up scarce resources while the poor can only stand by helplessly. What this adds up to is an indictment of developed nations, which evidently have lost sight of the goal of harmony and, even worse, actively interfere with the process. It sometimes seems as if Third World rhetoric has found its way into the textbook interpretations. There is some evidence to support this contention. At a UNESCO conference in 1974, the U.S. government was criticized for not having ratified a proposal to encourage "international attitudes and global perspective" among children. This proposal contains all the shibboleths about rich nations exploiting poor ones, American resistance to "genuine revolutionary movements," and the need to curtail Western imperialism. At UNESCO meetings such bastions of freedom as Afghanistan, Mongolia, and Poland have argued for "the *correct reflection* . . . of the history, culture, and civilization of the peoples of the world" (my emphasis). And in an instance of unparalleled arrogance and hypocrisy, the Soviet Union in 1983 declared that "textbooks must become instruments of peace." The National Education Association, using rhetoric similar to that of UNESCO meetings, pronounced favorably in its teacher guidebooks on the obligation of "rich" nations (read, Western states) to assist poor ones. Wittingly or unwittingly, the characterization of the United States, and by implication the other industrialized Western nations, as money-grubbing, selfish imperialists has found its way into many textbook interpretations of the world situation.

In the world portrayed in these texts the rich nations are "supposed" to assist the poor nations because the poor nations are unable to help themselves. Competition between or among states in the form of trade and market shares is considered an anachronism; "cooperation" is the wave of the future. And invariably economic progress is acceptable only if the rich nations recognize their responsibility to the poor states.

Outside of a limited vision for the United States, the ideologists have an expansive vision for the rest of the world. The world economy must grow, while ours must shrink. We should retreat to a simple way of life and in the process improve the standard of living for the poor in other nations.

Prentice-Hall's *The United States: Combined Edition* (1982) illustrates this point by noting:

> Raised on the gospel of progress, few wanted to be told that there were limits to the nation's capacities, powers, and natural resources; that they must lower their expectations and aspirations; that they would need to exercise self-discipline and be prepared to make sacrifices.

Another general concern of the ideologists is governance, particularly the belief that someone, somewhere, can and should decide difficult issues. No one can question the need to address serious matters, nor is the legitimacy of governments being called to account by me or the textbook authors. But what is routinely included in these books is an unanswered query such as "Who in a given country should decide whether to use technological improvements?" (Silver Burdett, *This Is Our World,* 1981) or "Who decides such questions as: How fast should new inventions be developed? How should scarce resources be allocated? How fast should new inventions be mass produced?" (Allyn & Bacon, *The Pageant of American History,* 1975). With the exception of one text, Ginn's *A History of the United States* (1981), there is no reminder that these problems and decisions regarding technology are not new. One could argue that the problems seem more intractable now than they once were, but they have all been considered before. Moreover, of what possible benefit is it to students to include a question that is not answered? Presumably the questions are designed to elicit thoughtful responses, but how can they when the foundation for discussion hasn't been established? At the risk of conjecture I regard these questions as consistent with the rest of the textual material. They can arouse potential readers but they don't illuminate the issues. The implication in these governance sections is that "the people have the power" but they are not making the decisions. Why they don't exercise this power or whether they have the power or who these people are or how governments operate is as vague after reading the texts as before reading them.

The concluding chapters in most of the texts that espouse heavy-handed ideological positions either cite words of hope that are unsubstantiated by the evidence presented or inspire fear through hauntingly prescient predictions. In the former category are the "flag-waving" conclusions seemingly at odds with what preceded them. This might be described as hedging your bets. Merrill's *Economics: Principles and Practices* (1981) notes: ". . . [A]ccording to our past, the United States most assuredly will have continued prosperity in the future." Harcourt Brace Jovanovich's *Rise of the American Nation* (1982) makes this point: "The American people have solved many immense problems during the course of their nation's history. They need only the will and commitment to meet the new challenges of the future." Although these statements are true, they are preceded by a description of Americans polluting their streams, befouling their air, destroying their cropland and forests, etc. In this context, it is hard to believe the positive claims are anything more than gratuitous.

In the category of "fear-provoking predictions" is one American history textbook that labels its last section "Crisis." Laidlaw's *A History of Our American Republic* (1981), which devotes considerable space to the idea of world government, ends with a reference to "the formation of a new political order," followed by a recommendation for a "case study" on the arms race. Presumably there is some connection between these matters in the mind of the authors and some relationship to the premise of building international harmony. But how we move to this new world order or what methods will be employed for reducing the arms race are not discussed. Is the new world order to be modeled on the United Nations? If so, will it be organized around one country, one vote? This would make Micronesia happy. Or should it be organized around the principle of one person, one vote? This would certainly please China. Or should it be one dollar, one vote? Obviously the method favored by the United States and Japan. In short, a generalized discussion of a new world order without considering the critical variables is a fairly worthless exercise. The same is true for a simple discussion of the "arms race." Is the race controlled by mutual understanding or by U.S. unilateral disarmament? If it is through mutual understanding, how do you punish violators of a treaty? What does the history of arms control agreements tell us about how reliable they are? Why doesn't the Laidlaw text, which makes the recommendation for a "case study" on arms control, consider the case of great-power agreements on ships during the 1920s? In short, these recommendations fall into the category of "educating" without responsibility.

Some texts conclude with "think pieces" designed to make students ponder over the assumptions in the text. Harcourt Brace Jovanovich's *American Civics* (1979) concludes with this statement: "Start thinking about what you can do to help keep the world a fit place for people." I can't argue with the recommendation, but the presumption that the world may not be a fit place for people in the future is not borne out by this text's unsubstantiated arguments. It is not enough to say that over-population, pollution, and the loss of cropland pose serious problems. There is an informed context for the discussion of these matters, and the authors have a responsibility to present it.

Then there are textbooks that offer "mixed benefits" statements about Western life-styles. Houghton Mifflin's *Unfinished Journey* (1983), which to its credit is one of the few texts that recognizes pessimism itself as a problem, concludes with a quotation by Peter Gay: "The world has not turned out the way the philosophers wished and half-expected it would. . . . We have known horrors, and may know horrors, that men of the enlightenment did not see in their nightmares." Then the textbook authors add:

But the present is also a time of hope and promise. Humanity possesses the intellectual and material resources to respond creatively to the challenges of the times. A failure of nerve, a loss of will, a listlessness of spirit, a sense of futility can destroy civilization. This is one of the lessons of history, perhaps the principal one.

Which theory are students expected to choose: horrors beyond their imagination or creative responses? Obviously the latter is the only reasonable choice, but do the students know this? Have the textbooks provided a context for creative responses, or do the textbooks downgrade imagination and instinctive good sense by setting the stage for despair? Is an ideological presentation the best way to discuss such complex issues?

There really is only one bottom line: Do textbooks help educate students to lead productive and enriching lives? On the basis of the evidence presented here, the answer is "No." To the extent that the texts encourage an unequivocally negative outlook or provide unsubstantiated arguments or think pieces that aren't thoughtful or questions that provoke without a context for answers, they are encouraging the miseducation of our students.

9

Conclusions

Today we need new utopian and anti-utopian concepts that look forward to super-industrialism, rather than backward to simpler societies.
Alvin Toffler, *Future Shock* (1970)

Conclusions

As late as the beginning of the nineteenth century, poverty was accepted as part of the natural order of things—a condition as endemic to society as disease, illness, and waste. It is illusory to believe that wealth or the "good life" was enjoyed by the bulk of mankind before the twentieth century. An elemental fact of history is that concern over the "quality of life" for the masses is a phenomenon of this century. One could justifiably argue that there are a great many things wealth does not buy, or emphasize the problems that accrue from putting excessive value on materialism, but that does not diminish the enormous accomplishment of having reduced poverty as a basic condition so that it is now the exception rather than the rule.

When T. S. Eliot in *The Love Song of J. Alfred Prufrock* plaintively asked, "Do I dare disturb the universe?" the response was predictably negative. But the universe has been disturbed. Mankind has explored, manipulated, and managed the Earth, its environs, its resources. We fly into space and we program even the smallest details with computers. We have evolved from a condition in which nature dictated the terms of human existence to a technical order in which nature has been largely harnessed to serve human needs.

This quest for recasting the relationship of humanity to nature is the essential story of our time. This quest may or may not be pursued indefinitely. But for now, at least, the human ability to manipulate the physical environment is enormous. Mankind has triumphed over nature in many areas where nature, if left unchecked, would not be conducive to the continued progress of mankind.

I make these apparently obvious claims because they are routinely ignored in the textbooks. Wealth is taken for granted, like the air we breathe. In fact, since the air we breathe is assumed to be polluted, clean air isn't taken for granted at all. That there may be a relationship between air pollution and the manufacture of goods that produce wealth is not studied very carefully; what is studied is the idea that if manufacturing produces air pollution, and air pollution is bad, manufacturing must be curtailed. (No one stops to consider what the effects of curtailment might be on national wealth and ultimately on the international economic system.) If this country wanted a virtually pollution-free environment, that might be possible. But the price would be either the elimination of those industries that produce pollutants (for example, lumber, chemicals, steel) or an enormous increase in the price of those industrial products to pay for cleaning. In the texts, however, wealth is not treated as a precarious endowment that can be affected by bad judgment or reduced through trade-offs for other values.

It is one thing to omit information and quite another to present inaccurate "facts." In reading the social studies texts one is put under the dizzying spell of doomsday predictions. In part this is a reflection of what pollsters tell us is the American mood of pessimism. The texts exploit and bring to the surface the subterranean fears of the populace. There are either explicitly apocalyptic visions of rich nations fighting poor ones in a war of survival or suggestions that environmental hazards may well doom us all.

Although I have conspicuously omitted any mention of nuclear war, the textbooks commonly note that mutual incineration is in the cards. In a new high school guide for New York City social studies teachers, a section from Jonathan Schell's *Fate of the Earth* is reprinted as a curriculum recommendation for nuclear issues discussion. Surely there is nothing wrong with assigning sections of Schell's book to students and teachers if this reading were accompanied by the assignment of a book with a different point of view—for example, Herman Kahn's *On Thermonuclear War;* Joyce Larson and William Bodie's *The Intelligent Layperson's Guide to the Nuclear Freeze and Peace Debate.*

There is no compelling reason to suggest—as Schell does—that deterrence can't work. As authors with a different viewpoint note, deterrence can be effective if this nation has the will to defend itself. In this context it translates into the maintenance of a nuclear force sufficient to discourage a first strike by the Soviet Union. But whether this argument is accepted is unimportant. The point is that it has at least as much validity as the Schell position and deserves to be included in any curriculum guide. That, however, isn't the case. Instead, Schell's nuclear "last gasp" rules the cultural roost, possibly even eclipsing its "eco-catastrophe" rival.

The apocalyptic possibilities that characterize textbook portrayals of the global society are carefully chosen so that the negative features of the present are factored into future predictions. Positive developments and much of the progress synonymous with historical evolution are virtually ignored.

The textbook view of people and society is static. "Adaptation" is a word rarely employed outside of biology books. Resources are finite; the human capacity to deal with problems is limited; a world view of the future (even based on computer extrapolation) is unimaginative. By inference, this is a passive world in which individual creativity and initiative play an insignificant role and where the dynamism and interaction inherent in society are essentially ignored. Instead the books present situations where one is almost forced to anticipate disaster, reduce risk, and protect oneself. Almost every problem is "life-threatening," almost every issue is beyond solution. It is as if we were all on the *Titanic* about to go down.

Maybe the dire predictions our textbooks emphasize will occur. In any case, one cannot be certain they won't. But the point to remember—the point that is usually excluded from discussion of the future—is that this civilization is as vulnerable (or invulnerable) to destruction as other civilizations. Societies in the past have survived volcanic explosions, war, decadence, and disorder. There is no reason to believe that these conditions can't exist again, as there is no reason to believe they must happen. Of these dire predictions it can be said only that the jury is out. Textbook authors should say that. They have a responsibility to point out potential hazards but also to illustrate that comparable issues have been dealt with before and that previous generations have survived.

History can provide many lessons; it can also provide perspective. It is precisely this perspective that our students require. With it "emergencies" become less tendentious, risks can be more appropriately weighed and evaluated. With perspective the gloom may seem less gloomy and the prospects for a bright future may appear somewhat brighter. In the present atmosphere, realism can be a healthy antidote to the pessimism that is the pervasive ideology. The question, of course, is how we get from here to there.

Bias will never be eliminated from textbooks, nor is that even desirable. Subjects such as history, future studies, economics, and political science are intrinsically biased since they present more than simply "the facts." They are theoretical disciplines that require a frame of reference. With economics, for example, theories of price, supply, and demand give facts context and make them comprehensible. Theories, however, unavoidably translate into bias. The very presentation of one idea as opposed to another reveals bias.

What contemporary textbooks require is not less bias but

more balance and perspective. The problem with this prescription is that it runs against the current of prevailing sentiments. Ideologists usually are not willing to consider another point of view.

Recently I spoke to a person concerned with the urban and rural planning for a major southern state. During the course of our conversation about environmentalism, she asked what I thought about strip mining. Since I have no well-formulated opinion on the subject, I said, "It depends on the circumstances. If the community regards the costs as acceptable after the costs and benefits are evaluated, it probably is worth doing." Her response to my comment was: "My dear Dr. London, that's nonsense. I accept the Aristotelian idea that we must live in harmony with nature. That covenant can't be broken through a utilitarian weighing of costs and benefits. Strip mining is wrong; it rapes the Earth. We must end it."

For this regional planner, "Thou shalt not defile the environment regardless of the human benefits" is the Eleventh Commandment. Unfortunately, it is this very messianic pose that permeates the textbooks and undermines a fair consideration of the issues. An inflexible concern for environmental purity often seems to transcend any other potential benefits.

It is odd that American education, which has traditionally been perceived as pragmatic and utilitarian—sometimes to a fault—now considers a pristine environment to be a high-priority national goal. One often hears that the trouble with the younger generation is that "it has not read the minutes of the last meeting," meaning that it has no real sense of history. I suspect students would benefit from a greater knowledge of history, but they would benefit at least as much from a balanced interpretation of contemporary affairs and from a pedagogical approach less laden with moralistic pronouncements.

It is at once amusing and distressing that the environmental preachers employ as symbols of their cause the deer deprived of food in the Grand Canyon or a lily pond strangulated by its own reproduction. Here is an illustration that confuses the flora and fauna in nature with human adaptability. What textbooks overlook and what *must* be noted is that human survival is an instinct modified by will and intelligence. We are neither deer, lilies, nor dinosaurs. The greatest error anyone can make about future projections of the human species is to confuse humans with plants and animals.

A contributor to this confusion is B. F. Skinner and his notion of determinism. The so-called science of experimental psychology has replaced a spuriously honorific notion of "man as God" with a Pavlovian idea of "man as dog." B. F. Skinner's cast-iron behaviorism confuses the responses of pigeons in a laboratory with the complex and serendipitous reactions of human beings in a manifestly unpredictable world. That mankind shares many basic needs and desires with animals—food, shelter, survival, and so on—is obvious. But unlike animals, people are occasionally willing to risk optimum comfort and security for the sake of values that are more prized than physical safety. Unlike animals, man is conscious of his approaching death and can often forestall peril through rational deliberation over alternative courses of action. Unlike animals, man's spirit can transcend physical and environmental limitations, creating a mastery over nature that accounts for both the creative and destructive potential in human decisions. For better or worse, man is an altogether unique being, projecting a power and imagination foreign to all other animals.

In describing present environmental problems as a reflection of the ecological system, many authors ignore the characteristics in human behavior that distinguish us from animals.

Behaviorism tries to replace the intangibles, the intuitive aspects of human decisions with the observation of empirical reactions to stimuli. But the causal links aren't usually explicit; the great breaks in the chain of causation are what characterize so much of human activity. To suggest that the exercise of will is a function of conditioning is to change human behavior into its base animal form. To suggest that people cannot influence nature and reorder the relationship between human beings and the world is to ignore the recent history of life on this globe.

Yet that is precisely what is going on. A whole generation has a fairly good sense of *how* things *do not* happen. Many students are obliged to learn what is either untrue or sadly misleading. In this context it is worth repeating what Joseph Schumpeter wrote in *Capitalism, Socialism and Democracy:*

> Perhaps the most striking feature of the picture is the extent to which the modern bourgeoisie, besides educating its own enemies, allows itself in turn to be educated by them. It absorbs the slogans of current radicalism and seems quite willing to undergo a process of conversion hostile to its very existence.

One illustration may be used in this regard. It is argued in most of the texts that the gap between rich and poor states has been widening—a point I discussed earlier. However, in not one source is the continuum or spectrum of income levels examined, or the extraordinary success stories in the developing world cited. The point the texts make is that our aid is insufficient to narrow the gap and that we've got to do more or pay the consequences. But instead of emphasizing the need for massive aid and a criticism of U.S. foreign-aid policy, it might prove useful if textbook writers considered such economic conditions as trade, markets, economic growth, and other catalysts for self-generated projects. Curiously, these conditions for economic development also are usually excluded.

What difference does all this make? Even if one agrees that social studies textbooks misrepresent issues, does this cause irreparable harm to high school students, or is this filtered out of their minds as easily as logarithms and differential equations? The problem with these misrepresentations is that they reflect a fervor, an almost religious belief that we must do something to protect ourselves from our contemporaries who don't see the light. Robert Nisbet argues, "After Christianity and modern socialism, environmentalism is the third great wave of redemptive struggle in Western history." If he is right—and I believe the evidence suggests he is—we are encouraging a generation of students to be intolerant about matters over which they have been systematically misled. Their emotions have been exercised and their mental faculties coerced. The students are asked to emphasize, to suffer, and to feel guilty with only the most cursory understanding of why this should be so. How can these guilt-ridden teenagers of today—seeking redemption through their concern over pollution and poverty—possibly be the clear-headed and objective decisionmakers of tomorrow? This is a new form of demonology that forces upon us the conclusion that sacrifice is the highest duty to our fellow man.

As Julian Simon has pointed out in his several attempts to "set the record straight," in a short period a mass movement has been organized to enact environmental and population policies based on erroneous claims and faulty research. Yet no organizations or media programs are designed to present accurate information, just as very few textbooks present these issues correctly. As Simon notes:

These activities already have caused misallocation of natural resources in the United States, sapping of the national will, deterioration of public morale and loss of confidence (with consequent reduction in risk investment) in the business community.

No one can say with any assurance how this will end, but any movement fueled by misleading claims and narrowly defined interests may have drastic consequences. It is already widely believed that there are relatively few risks worth taking. The potential result of such a belief obviously is stagnation and paralysis. Alfred North Whitehead's claim that "the business of the future is danger" has been rejected in favor of timidity and restitution—making up for the careless, wasteful misdeeds of the past and present. This belief explains why so many Americans believe we must begin a zealous redistribution of our wealth to assuage our guilt.

What the textbook writers ignore is any mention of the promise of a new age that is already visible on the horizon. This is an age where medical breakthroughs will turn dreams into reality: Life expectancy may approach ninety by the year 2000; there will be a revolution in health care, from replaceable parts (prostheses) to recombinant genetic pharmaceuticals capable of eliminating most viral diseases. There is likely to be a shift to even greater leisure time than at present. A new era of exotic energy choices at relatively competitive prices is not far off. Better, stronger, safer materials, especially plastics, will replace many fibers. And travel will be fast, comfortable, low-cost, and easy: The advertising claim of "leave the driving to us" may be a reality, with the "us" being efficient machines operated by computers. Worldwide communications in "real time" will be achieved through a Dick Tracy-like wrist receiver.

Although many will not find these changes desirable, they will generally improve material conditions as well as the quality of life, even as they extract a price. For example, the ease of worldwide communications may be viewed as an infringement on privacy; a longer life-span will impose pressure on government to provide social services for the elderly.

As I've suggested many times before, economic development has both costs and benefits. The future is not inevitably rosy. Hazards undoubtedly await us, and the magnitude of some problems cannot be anticipated. But the point worth noting is that our textbooks choose to place heavy emphasis on the hazards and problems while subordinating the potential promise and hope. Yet students—everyone—require hope to live. A future dominated by gloom is not only unappealing, it is also unlivable.

Our textbooks tend to present a variety of options and scenarios of despair. They marshal fallacious (or certainly undocumented) arguments to justify their claims and moralize about issues open to many interpretations. Outdated, inaccurate, biased, and absurd claims have entered our children's texts and, at least for the moment, nothing is being done about it.

What can be done? For students and parents concerned about the issues raised in this book, there are several ways to proceed. When the doom catechism appears in the texts and in classroom discussion, it is imperative that one asks for the source and the ideological persuasion of the author of these assertions. Over the past few years there has emerged a cadre of "gloom professionals" such as Paul Ehrlich and Barry Commoner. They see their role as vigilant surveyors of imminent doom. Their investment in certain observations makes them somewhat less than dispassionate. For these propagandists a failed fuse on a spaceship to the moon is enough to describe the voyage as a failure. It is therefore incumbent on those who care about such matters to put the record straight, which usually means attempting to counter the arguments of the environmental doomsayers with balanced presentations.

To do this, several key questions must be put to the advocates of gloomy predictions, questions as value-laden as their assumptions:

• If environmental damage is so significant and the cause of many diseases, why have life expectancy rates been steadily increasing?

• If the world is divided into rich states and poor states, and if the gap between them continues to widen, how can you explain the emergence of a middle class in much of the so-called Third World?

• If we are running out of materials, why, with few exceptions, has the price of minerals decreased when demand for them is high?

• If our environment is so badly polluted, how do you account for the reduction in hydrocarbons and carbon monoxide in the atmosphere?

The answers to these questions reveal that things are not entirely as bleak as we have been led to believe. Clearly an advocate will try to evade the issue by discussing the potential for catastrophe. But catastrophe always is possible; the point is whether it is probable. Teachers have an obligation to be fair, even when they cannot always be objective. Fairness in this context means providing as much reliable information as possible and avoiding the zealous pursuit of only one point of view.

This brings me to an absurd but nonetheless revealing example of what several teachers in a southern state considered fairness. In a discussion about demography, I illustrated the exaggerated predictions about population based on projections in 1965. The projections were made by Paul Ehrlich, and the corrections were made by the United Nations population statisticians in 1982. After I had completed my remarks, one teacher raised his hand and said, "In this school system we believe in fairness; if you're going to present U.N. statistics then you should also present Paul Ehrlich." I thought that this fellow must also teach the Earth is flat to be fair to the proponents that it is round. One isn't being fair to students by balancing an accurate claim with an inaccurate one.

Obviously the problem with fairness interpreted in this way is that it soon becomes <u>fatuous relativism</u>. Every idea, no matter how demonstrably true, will have to be balanced by its opposite, no matter how demonstrably false. What I propose is <u>the bright light of careful observation focused on unsubstantiated claims or arguments that don't square with common sense.</u> Surely at times those unsubstantiated claims and seemingly odd opinions will be true. But the process of withholding judgment is more important than either the justification or the proof of falseness.

It is useful to consider the careful critique of *The Global 2000 Report* done for the American Association for the Advancement of Science by Julian Simon and Herman Kahn. Although the report discusses impending ecological disaster and a world more crowded, less stable, and more vulnerable to disruption than under present conditions, the critique claims "the overall picture it paints . . . is fundamentally wrong partly because it relies on nonfacts and partly because it misinterprets the correct facts it does present." Among the chief findings in the critique are:

- Overblown predictions of air and water pollution
- A lack of evidence for the rapid loss of animal species
- Rapidly rising life expectancy that may be the best indicator of scientific and economic success
- An improving food supply, even with many hungry people

worldwide
- A climate that does not show signs of unusual change
- Mineral resources that are less scarce rather than more scarce because of technological advances
- An absence of evidence that oil prices will rise in the near term

The authors hastily note that not everything will be positive in the future. But for the most part they are heartened by aggregate global and U.S. trends that are improving rather than deteriorating.

The question is how two reports relying on ostensibly the same data can arrive at such different conclusions. It is not surprising, of course, that two people examining the same evidence can derive very different views. What is interesting in this instance is the response of supporters of *The Global 2000 Report* to charges that their alarming predictions were exaggerated. The replies I have heard most often are: "We cannot be complacent in the face of a great potential threat to our existence" and "We owe it to our children and grandchildren to give them an ecological system intact." These, I might add, have become standard arguments in the debate and often are employed as a justification for "exaggerated" reportage. Yet both arguments are misleading and skirt the essential issue.

Almost everyone feels obliged to disown complacency. This is an attitude I share when there is a compelling reason to avoid complacency. But if I am asked to endorse "cry wolf" predictions of doom that have little basis in experience and are unpersuasive in their argument, only to fend off complacency, then complacency is the appropriate response. When several of my students tell me that they unfairly received "B" in a course instead of "A" but can provide no evidence to substantiate their argument other than that they "need" an "A" to get into graduate school, I am consistently unpersuaded. Similarly, some of the environmentalist arguments are so unpersuasive as to evoke complacency. Why should I be made to feel guilty if I do not act when the evidence doesn't indicate action is warranted? If I were to act on the basis of a faulty prediction that never materializes, I might condemn myself, my family, and my friends to unwarranted deprivation. One sure road to poverty is to spend your money and efforts on events that do not occur.

Then there is the "we owe it to our children" argument. This strikes a responsive chord with every concerned parent. But it too usually is a bogus claim. The best endowment any parent can leave his or her child is not natural resources. When I concern myself about what kind of endowment I want to leave my daughters, it usually takes the form of education. This is a resource that lasts a long time and—assuming a solid analytical foundation—is adaptable to many unforeseen contingencies. However, to afford this education I must use my energies and investments now to plan for my children's legacy. This neither takes the form of complacency, nor does it suggest the maintenance of an unspoiled environment. On the contrary, the best thing I can do for my children is use present resources so I can give them a genuinely meaningful future.

This doesn't mean I ignore a duty to nature. As a fisherman and camper I deeply appreciate what nature can provide. I do not advocate capricious exploitation of natural resources. This view, however, has little to do with future generations of Londons. I often ask myself if it is morally right to deprive myself and those children now living for the sake of descendants a century away. If morality is based on obligations to those around me, do I concentrate my efforts on those in some distant future, or do I fix my gaze on people with whom my life intersects? The answer, I believe, is self-evident. It is also worth recalling that revolutionaries have always argued that we must endure hardships now for the sake of future generations. This usually is a prescription for hardship now and hardship later. If the spirit of a nation is undermined now, what makes us think it can be restored later?

George Will has argued that "all education is moral because learning conditions conduct." The character of our children is very much influenced by the behavior preached as well as the behavior practiced. In fact, as both moralists and pragmatists know, education involves a great deal more than conveying factual information. Schools are socializing agents. Students are expected to be punctual, reasonably polite (the word "reasonably" speaks volumes about the modification in manners), and concerned about the feelings of fellow students, to name only several of the untold social lessons taught in schools. Students are also expected to weigh evidence, be critical-minded, and reserve judgment until all the arguments can be considered. These are the traits of a trained mind. They are part of the process of learning.

The problem with this analysis is that too few educators concern themselves with the social dimensions of education, and most educators, while they give lip service to the training of the mind, observe this more in the breach than in the practice. Consequently, classroom exchanges resemble television news broadcasts: "I have a crisis to report today that should concern you deeply." As I've already noted, most of the announced crises aren't crises at all. Perhaps Alexis de Tocqueville's observation on American public opinion applies to our contemporary schools: "I know of no country in which there is so little true independence of mind and freedom of discussion as in America." It is difficult for a student to withstand the pressures of peer group opinion; it is sometimes more difficult to withstand the force of teacher opinion and textbook interpretations. Education certainly is not public opinion, albeit norms do influence the character of our schools. When consensus emerges through media presentations, teacher attitudes, peer pressure, and textbook analysis, it is very hard for the typical student to oppose the tide of popular opinion. But that is precisely where we stand at the moment. Unless a student is well armed with information and confident about his or her point of view, the student cannot possibly challenge prevailing sentiments. John Stuart Mill once argued: "If all mankind minus one were of one opinion . . . mankind would be no more justified in silencing that one person than he, if he had the power, would be justified in silencing mankind. . . ." Thoreau expressed it differently but made essentially the same point: "When you are right, you represent a majority of one." The problem, of course, is that most teachers believe themselves right, and most students believe it, too. The result is that many people in our culture are not silenced, but silence themselves through ignorance.

This is not a moral judgment but a reminder that as parents we should maintain a vigil over what our students learn and how they are being taught so that those values we care about are sustained and the training of the mind is fostered. A consensual view that Western industrial man is avaricious, egotistical, and selfish, while his counterparts in the Third World are noble and worthy is a pernicious lie. Yet this is precisely one of the myths continually perpetuated in our schools and in our textbooks. It is precisely the kind of opinion that can have a harmful effect on our students by misleading them about the world they will inherit.

At this point my detractors will raise the argument of chauvinism. That criticism, however, misses the point. I am not arguing here for unvarnished patriotism in our schools, although that would be a healthy antidote to the widespread anti-Americanism.

I am suggesting that balanced opinion requires a realistic program about what this nation has done and what it stands for. Mae West said, "I'm no angel." Indeed she wasn't, and neither are we. But Americans certainly are not as thoughtless and as greedy as textbooks often characterize us. The redeeming qualities of Western culture and American influence should be understood and appreciated. To make youngsters feel shame about our national heritage is a crime whose punishment will unfold in the years to come.

Let me then turn to several specific recommendations.

1. Examine the textbooks your children are reading, not because you are launching into a censorship crusade but because you may be able to raise questions that inspire class discussion.
2. Give your son or daughter the necessary information to challenge teachers and texts and to bolster his or her confidence in doing so.
3. Encourage independent research through questions such as "How do you know that is true?" "Is there a respectable counter view you can cite?"
4. Anticipate discussion by postulating issues such as "Is the rich-poor dichotomy in the text an accurate description of world conditions?" "Is pollution more acute today than 50 years ago?" "Are we running out of natural resources?" "Is famine more widespread than it was a century ago?" "How does one measure the quality of life?"
5. Pose two different points of view and have them both considered. For example, have your children evaluate the following two statements, the first from *The Global 2000 Report* and the second from the Simon/Kahn critique.

Our conclusions, summarized in the pages that follow, are disturbing. They indicate the potential for global problems of alarming proportions by the year 2000. Environmental, resource, and population stresses are intensifying and will increasingly determine the quality of human life on our planet. These stresses are already severe enough to deny many millions of people basic needs for food, shelter, health, and jobs, or any hope for betterment. At the same time, the earth's carrying capacity—the ability of biological systems to provide resources for human needs—is eroding. The trends reflected in the Global 2000 suggest strongly a progressive degradation and impoverishment of the earth's natural resource base.

Our conclusions are reassuring, though not grounds for complacency. Global problems due to physical conditions (as distinguished from those caused by institutional and political conditions) are always possible, but are likely to be less pressing in the future than in the past. Environmental, resource, and population stresses are diminishing, and with the passage of time will have less influence than now upon the quality of human life on our planet. These stresses have in the past always caused many people to suffer from lack of food, shelter, health, and jobs, but the trend is toward less rather than more of such suffering. Especially important and noteworthy is the dramatic trend toward longer and healthier life through all the world. Because of increases in knowledge, the earth's "carrying capacity" has been increasing throughout the decades and centuries and millennia to such an extent that the term "carrying capacity" has by now no useful meaning. These trends strongly suggest a progressive improvement and enrichment of the earth's natural resource base, and of mankind's lot on earth.

In the last analysis, we should want our children to be able to develop independent opinions molded by thoughtful analysis and normative judgments. If this review of textbooks can lead us back to this goal, it will have more than achieved my expectations. Then, even if not all our children grow up to be optimists, at least many of them will be realists.

Epilogue

S ince completing the research for this book there has been a plethora of committee reports, news programs, and editorials devoted to American schools. "Excellence in education" has emerged on the political scene as a comet moving very quickly, generating some light, and prompting a lot of self-evident discussion. The media have suddenly discovered what most people have always known: If the schools are excessively permissive and unstructured, students won't do much work. If our expectations of performance are low, student performance will be low. And if our teachers are not well prepared to teach, little will be taught. Any taxi driver in New York or grocer in Indianapolis could have made the same observation.

What has affected education over the past two decades, what I call in shorthand fashion the "sixties contagion" of "do your own thing" psychology, has had its effect on undermining the discipline needed in the teaching-learning process. That lack of discipline breeds students who don't do their work, teachers who don't require much work (and who themselves don't always do their "homework"), and schools that become playpens for the self-indulgent or day-care centers for those whose parents work. There is no mystery about the problem.

In this atmosphere it is understandable that rhetoric easily can substitute for hardheaded analysis. Slogans are not limited to catchy phrases created by the advertising world; they have become the medium for normal discourse. When my colleagues at the university tell me to "open up" or "lay it all out," they are not referring to a ripe watermelon or my sleeping bag. The contamination of language is symptomatic of a lot of fuzzy thinking.

Educators are now forced to pay a very high price for their abdication of responsibility. It is no coincidence that the slide in academic standards is associated with the emergence of very questionable hypotheses about our environment, economic development, and the future. Who was there to blow the whistle? Who was willing to do the hard, painstaking job of reviewing the catch phrases that capture our attention but are devoid of substance and are sometimes inaccurate?

Surely the schools are not alone in promulgating or in coping with this problem. Government agencies take their own unsubstantiated reports seriously and subsequently introduce policies that sometimes have had a deleterious effect on the nation. For example, block grants to recycling centers (which process waste at much higher cost than ordinary waste disposal centers) were based on an erroneous estimate of environmental damage caused by garbage. Federally imposed natural-gas contracts that locked in artificially high prices ignored the conditions in the marketplace that influence demand when the price is higher than the public is willing to pay. And federal regulations mandating fuel economy measures in automobiles forced redesign costs on manufacturers at the very time the automobile industry was already in financial trouble.

Every American has a stake in promoting clear thinking. That always has been the presumptive goal of our education system. The problem is that we've let conditions slide. We let facile statements substitute for hard analysis, and we let undocumented, inflammatory rhetoric find its way into our texts. For these bad judgments we will pay a price in miseducated youths. Because schools are local institutions subject to parental influence, much can be accomplished immediately when there is the will to do so. There isn't that much to do. The application of commonsense standards of "fair play" and "balanced argument" will go a long way toward correcting the lies our students are routinely taught.

Bibliography of Textbooks Reviewed

Addison-Wesley, *An American History*, 1981 (Rebecca Brooks Gruver)
Addison-Wesley, *Essentials of Economics and Free Enterprise*, 1982 (Richard M. Hodgetts and Terry L. Smart)
Addison-Wesley, *Our Economy: How It Works*, 1980 (Elmer U. Clawson)
Allyn & Bacon, *The Eastern Hemisphere*, 1983 (Harold D. Drummond and James W. Hughes)
Allyn & Bacon, *Magruder's American Government*, 1982 (William A. McClenaghan, author of revision)
Allyn & Bacon, *Our World and Its Peoples*, 1981 (Edward R. Kolevzon and John A. Heine)
Allyn & Bacon, *The Pageant of American History*, 1975 (Gerald Leinwand)
Allyn & Bacon, *The Pageant of World History*, 1983 (Gerald Leinwand)
Allyn & Bacon, *The Western Hemisphere*, 1983 (Harold D. Drummond and James W. Hughes)
Follett, *Our World Today*, 1983 (Phillip Bacon and James B. Kracht)
Follett, *World Geography*, 1983 (Herbert H. Gross)
Ginn, *America's Heritage*, 1982 (Margaret Stimmann Branson)
Ginn, *Exploring World Cultures*, 1981 (Esko E. Newhill and Umberto La Paglia)
Ginn, *A History of the United States*, 1981 (Daniel J. Boorstin and Brooks Mather Kelly with Ruth Frankel Boorstin)
Ginn, *Our Common Heritage: A World History*, 1981 (Daniel Roselle)

Ginn, *Economics and the American Free-Enterprise System*, 1983 (Jack Abramowitz, Roy Adkins, and J. H. Rogers)

Globe, *Exploring World History*, 1983 (Sol Holt and John R. O'Connor)

Globe, *The New Exploring: A Changing World*, 1980 (Melvin Schwartz and John O'Connor)

Harcourt Brace Jovanovich, *American Civics*, 1979 (William H. Hartley and William S. Vincent)

Harcourt Brace Jovanovich, *The Development of American Economic Life* (paperback), 1978 (Robert L. Heilbroner with Aaron Singer)

Harcourt Brace Jovanovich, *Free Enterprise in America* (paperback), 1977 (Andrew Hacker)*

Harcourt Brace Jovanovich, *The Impact of the Industrial Revolution* (paperback), 1978 (Nicholas B. Fessenden)*

Harcourt Brace Jovanovich, *Men and Nations: A World History*, 1975 (Anatole G. Mazour and John M. Peoples)

Harcourt Brace Jovanovich, *Rise of the American Nation*, 1977 and 1982 (Lewis Paul Todd and Merle Curti)

Harper & Row, *Faces of America: A History of the United States*, 1982 (R. M. Smith, E. D. Levy, and M. H. Brown)

Harper & Row, *Modern American History: The Search for Identity*, 1981 (John Edward Wiltz)

Harper & Row, *A People and a Nation*, 1981 (Clarence L. Ver Steeg and Richard Hofstadter)

Holt, Rinehart & Winston, *World Geography Today*, 1980 (Saul Israel, Douglas L. Johnson, and Denis Wood)

Holt, Rinehart & Winston, *People and Our World: A Study of World History*, 1981 (Allan O. Kownslar and Terry L. Smart)

Holt, Rinehart & Winston, *People, Places, and Change: An Introduction to Geography, History, and Cultures*, 1981 (Leonard Berry, Richard B. Ford, and Norman Carls)

Holt, Rinehart & Winston, *The American Way*, 1979 (Nancy W. Bauer)

Holt, Rinehart & Winston, *People and Our Country*, 1982 (Norman K. Risjord and Terry L. Haywoode)

Houghton Mifflin, *The American Economy: Analysis, Issues, Principles*, 1983 (Roy J. Sampson and Ira Marienhoff)

Houghton Mifflin, *Geography*, 1982 (Arthur Getis and Judith M. Getis)

Houghton Mifflin, *This Is America's Story*, 1983 (H. B. Wilder, R. P. Ludlum, and H. McC. Brown)

Houghton Mifflin, *Unfinished Journey*, 1983 (Marvin Perry et al.)

Laidlaw, *The Challenge of Freedom*, 1982 (R. Sobel, R. LaRaus, L. A. DeLeon, and H. P. Morris)

Laidlaw, *A History of Our American Republic*, 1981 (Glenn M. Linden et al.)

Laidlaw, *Free Enterprise—The American Economic System*, 1981 (Robert F. Smith, Michael W. Watts, and Vivian D. Hogan)

Lippincott, *The Human Expression: A History of Peoples and Their Cultures*, 1977 (Paul Thomas Welty)

Bibliography of Textbooks Reviewed

Macmillan, *Global Geography*, 1981 (Preston E. James and Nelda Davis)

Macmillan, *History of a Free People*, 1981 (Henry W. Bragdon and Samuel P. McCutchen)

Macmillan, *Modern Times* (paperback), 1983 (Carlton J. H. Hayes, Margareta Faissler, and Judith Walsh)

McGraw-Hill, *American Government*, 1980 (Allan O. Kownslar and Terry L. Smart)

McGraw-Hill, *Civics, Citizens and Society*, 1980 (Allan O. Kownslar and Terry L. Smart)

Merrill, *Economics: Principles and Practices*, 1981 (James E. Brown and Harold A. Wolf)

Merrill, *Global Insights: People and Cultures*, 1980 (Mounir A. Farah et al.)

Prentice-Hall, *American Government: Comparing Political Experiences*, 1979 (Judith Gillespie and Stuart Lazarus)

Prentice-Hall, *The Economic Problem*, 1981 (Robert L. Heilbroner and Lester C. Thurow)

Prentice-Hall, *The Future of the Environment*, 1977 (Judith G. Hellfach)

Prentice-Hall, *The United States: Combined Edition*, 1982 (Winthrop D. Jordan et al.)

Prentice-Hall, *The United States: A History of the Republic*, 1981 (James West Davidson and Mark H. Lytle)

Prentice-Hall, *World History: Patterns of Civilization*, 1983 (Burton F. Beers)

Rand McNally (distributed by Houghton Mifflin), *Geography and World Affairs*, 1976 (Stephen B. Jones and Marion Fisher Murphy)

Rand McNally, *The Promise of Democracy: The Grand Experiment*, 1978 (Henry F. Graff and Paul Bohannan)

Scott, Foresman, *America! America!* 1982 (L. J. Buggey, G. A. Danzer, C. L. Mitsakos, and C. F. Risinger)

Scott, Foresman, *The American Dream* (readings), 1980 (Lew Smith)*

Scott, Foresman, *The Developing World: Poverty, Growth and Rising Expectations* (paperback), 1976 (James D.Calderwood)*

Scott, Foresman, *Invitation to Economics*, 1982 (Lawrence Wolken and Janet Glocker)

Scott, Foresman, *Land and People: A World Geography*, 1982 (Gerald A. Danzer and Albert J. Larson)

Scott, Foresman, *Living World History*, 1982 (T. Walter Wallbank and Arnold Schrier)

Scott, Foresman, *People on Earth: A World Geography*, 1983 (Dorothy W. Drummond and Robert R. Drummond)

Scott, Foresman, *History and Life: The World and Its People*, 1982 (T. Walter Wallbank, Arnold Schrier, Donna Maier, and Patricia Gutierrez-Smith)

Silver Burdett, *America and Americans, Vol. II: From Reconstruction to the Present*, 1983 (H. J. Bass, G. A. Billias, and E. J. Lapansky)

*Statistical information on the textbooks reviewed does not include this book.

Silver Burdett, *Our American Heritage,* 1979,* 1983 (H. J. Bass, G. A. Billias, and
   E. J. Lapansky)
Silver Burdett, *This Is Our World*, 1981 (George H. Kimble)
Silver Burdett, *World Geography*, 1980 (Norman J. G. Pounds)

*Statistical information on the textbooks reviewed does not include this book.

Index

Index